ASIAN ECONOMIC AND P
FOOD AND BEVERAGE CONSU

FRUIT IN JAPAN

POLICIES
AND ISSUES

ASIAN ECONOMIC AND POLITICAL ISSUES

Additional books in this series can be found on Nova's website under the Series tab.

Additional E-books in this series can be found on Nova's website under the E-book tab.

FOOD AND BEVERAGE CONSUMPTION AND HEALTH

Additional books in this series can be found on Nova's website under the Series tab.

Additional E-books in this series can be found on Nova's website under the E-book tab.

ASIAN ECONOMIC AND POLITICAL ISSUES
FOOD AND BEVERAGE CONSUMPTION AND HEALTH

FRUIT IN JAPAN

POLICIES
AND ISSUES

PAUL C. BRADLEY
EDITOR

Nova Science Publishers, Inc.
New York

Additional color graphics may be available in the e-book version of this book.

LIBRARY OF CONGRESS CATALOGING-IN-PUBLICATION DATA

Fruit in Japan : policies and issues / editor, Paul C. Bradley.
p. cm.
Includes index.
ISBN 978-1-61761-115-5 (softcover)
1. Fruit trade--Japan. 2. Orange industry--Japan. I. Bradley, Paul C.
HD9256.J32F78 2009
338.1'740952--dc22
                                    2010026929

Published by Nova Science Publishers, Inc. ✦ *New York*

CONTENTS

Preface   **vii**

Chapter 1   Fruit Policies in Japan   **1**
                 United States Dept. of Agriculture

Chapter 2   The Japanese Market for Oranges   **31**
                 United States Dept. of Agriculture

Chapter 3   Declining Orange Consumption in Japan
                 (Generational Changes or Something Else?)   **47**
                 Hiroshi Mori, Dennis Clason, Kimiko Ishibashi,
                 William D. Gorman and John Dyck

Chapter Sources   **79**

Index   **81**

PREFACE

Japan is a large market for fruits and its consumers spend $10 billion per year (wholesale value) on fresh and preserved fruits. The United States, the second-largest foreign supplier of fruits to Japan, sent about $450 million in fruit exports to Japan in 2009, 10 percent of total U.S. fruit exports. Japanese government policies regarding this large market affect U.S. fruit exports and offer a point of comparison for other developed countries. Consumption of traditionally important fruits, such as citrus fruits and apples, has been declining and expenditures on fruits for consumption at home have decreased. This book examines Japan's policies that protect and regulate its agricultural markets. Japan's policies affect existing trade patterns and are relevant to the current round of global trade negotiations conducted by the World Trade Organization (WTO).

Chapter 1- Government programs and subsidies regulate and support Japan's large fruit-production sector, bolstering farm incomes and output levels. Supply-management programs that target annual production levels for some fruits, in order to maintain market prices, contribute to higher prices for consumers, although other programs aim to increase fruit consumption. Japan's tariffs and phytosanitary measures also create barriers to fruit consumption and limit imports. Producers in the United States, a major fruit supplier to Japan, could benefit from reduced barriers.

Chapter 2- Japan is a large market for U.S. oranges, and most of Japan's orange consumption is supplied by U.S. exports. Orange consumption and imports grew until 1994, but have declined since. Demographic shifts are linked to changing orange consumption: older birth cohorts eat more oranges, and younger ones eat fewer oranges; within each cohort, consumption increases with age. Income changes appear not to be major factors in the decline in orange consumption, but price changes appear to be potentially important. A downward trend in consumption, not explained by the demographic variables, prices, or income, may continue in the future.

Chapter 3- Japan is a leading market for U.S. oranges. Since 1995, orange consumption in Japan has declined. This report summarizes an analysis of household survey data to assess various factors that may be related to the decline. Consumption of oranges in Japan differs markedly across generations, with younger generations (cohorts) eating fewer oranges than older generations. However, within generations, as individuals in Japan grow older, they eat more oranges. On balance, the effects on consumption associated with aging and birth cohort membership are mostly offsetting. Orange prices affect consumption levels, but household income does not. Even after the analysis accounts for price and demographic variables, a strong downward trend is evident in orange consumption in Japan. Results suggest that orange consumption could decline even more in the future.

In: Fruit in Japan: Policies and Issues
Editors: Paul C. Bradley

ISBN: 978-1-61761-115-5
© 2010 Nova Science Publishers, Inc.

Chapter 1

FRUIT POLICIES IN JAPAN

United States Dept. of Agriculture

ABSTRACT

Government programs and subsidies regulate and support Japan's large fruit-production sector, bolstering farm incomes and output levels. Supply-management programs that target annual production levels for some fruits, in order to maintain market prices, contribute to higher prices for consumers, although other programs aim to increase fruit consumption. Japan's tariffs and phytosanitary measures also create barriers to fruit consumption and limit imports. Producers in the United States, a major fruit supplier to Japan, could benefit from reduced barriers.

Keywords: Japan, fruits, policies, production, subsidies, insurance, farm markets, tariffs, phytosanitary measures

ACKNOWLEDGMENTS

The authors gratefully acknowledge the review and comments of Molly Garber, Lewrene Glaser, Sophia Huang, Gary Lucier, Mary Anne Normile, Agnes Perez, and Susan Pollack, Economic Research Service; Hyunok Lee, University of California at Davis; Thomas Marsh, Washington State

University; William Gorman and Hiroshi Mori, New Mexico State University; Carol Goodloe, Office of the Chief Economist; and Reed Blauer and Shari Kosco, Foreign Agricultural Service. Editorial and design support was provided by Angela Anderson.

INTRODUCTION

Japan is a large market for fruits and its consumers spend $10 billion per year (wholesale value) on fresh and preserved fruits.[1] The United States, the second-largest foreign supplier of fruits to Japan, sent about $450 million in fruit exports to Japan in 2009—10 percent of total U.S. fruit exports (table 1).[2] Japanese Government policies regarding this large market affect U.S. fruit exports and offer a point of comparison for other developed countries, including the United States. This report is one in a series examining Japan's policies that protect and regulate its agricultural markets. Japan's policies affect existing trade patterns and are relevant to the current round of global trade negotiations conducted by the World Trade Organization (WTO).

Fruit demand in Japan appears to be declining. Japan's population, currently at about 127 million people, has also begun to decrease. Consumption of traditionally important fruits, such as citrus fruits and apples, has been declining, while consumption of some minor fruits, such as blueberries, has increased. Expenditures on fruits for consumption at home have decreased (figure 1). Japanese consumers are increasing their purchases of food away from home, but data on fruit consumption in restaurants and other venues are not available. Consumer prices for fruits have been stable, both in absolute terms and relative to the general price index, except for a spike in 2007 (figure 2).[3] Although not a growing market, Japan's fruit consumption remains large and economically significant.

Fruit production, by volume, declined about 20 percent from the 3-year average for 1994-96 to the average for 2004-06. Japan produces many fruit crops, benefiting from the climatic variation, both in latitude and in elevation above sea level, that the long string of mountainous islands offers. The leading fruit produced in Japan, by volume, is the mikan tangerine (or unshu), followed by apples, melons, pears, persimmons, grapes, strawberries, and peaches (table 2). The planted area and production of these fruits have gradually declined in recent years. Cherries are one of the few fruits in Japan with recent growth in area planted.

Table 1. U.S. fruit exports to Japan, 2004-08

	2004	2005	2006	2007	2008	2009	Average 2007-09	Japan tariff or tariff range
	1,000 U.S. dollars[1]							*Percent*
Grapefruit, fresh	120,234	65,542	97,498	139,426	99,816	97,436	112,226	10
Cherries, all forms[2]	85,521	86,935	58,838	62,484	67,636	70,092	66,737	8.5-17
Lemons, fresh	33,997	34,973	36,747	81,021	66,646	47,261	64,976	0
Oranges, fresh	50,987	58,518	67,473	41,893	71,747	61,322	58,321	16-32
Strawberries, all forms[2]	39,466	32,829	34,894	34,311	38,251	30,531	34,364	6-12
Raisins	28,756	30,805	27,101	30,557	34,328	30,531	31,805	1.2
Prunes	34,539	30,746	31,624	31,528	28,072	28,172	29,257	2.4
Blueberries, all forms[2]	22,457	25,609	24,490	26,693	28,098	22,014	25,784	6-12
Grapes, fresh	7,283	4,870	7,774	5,652	4,670	5,898	5,407	7.8-17
Melons, except watermelons	5,936	6,115	4,970	5,250	6,667	7,591	6,503	6-12
Other fruit, except juices	54,462	50,245	51,407	45,821	46,861	47,435	46,524	0-25
Total	483,638	427,187	442,816	504,636	492,792	448,283	481,904	

[1] Nominal dollars, not adjusted for inflation.
[2] "All forms" means fresh, frozen, dried, and otherwise preserved.
Source: ERS calculations based on data from Foreign Agricultural Trade of the United States database and table 4.

From 1994-96 to 2004-06, the quantity of fruits and nuts that Japan imported grew by almost 9 percent. Foreign producers often have advantages, such as low labor costs, that make imports competitive with Japan's domestic products. Japan does not have extensive areas suitable for tropical fruits, and its high humidity limits some fruit production. Japan's orchards and fields tend to be smaller than those in some exporting nations, both for topographic and historical reasons, potentially limiting Japan's ability to achieve economies of size.

Bananas are Japan's largest fruit import, by volume, followed by citrus fruits (table 2). Banana imports have remained relatively stable since 1999, while citrus fruit imports have declined since 1994. Pineapples are among the few fresh fruits with increasing import levels. Frozen fruit import volume grew until 2005, but has remained stable since. The Philippines have become the largest source for Japan's fruit imports (40 percent of value in 2008), followed by the United States (25 percent). Other countries supply small shares of the import market, but collectively provide almost 35 percent of Japan's imports (figure 3).

Japanese fruit farms face a variety of structural problems:

- More aging farmers and fewer new farmers;
- Inefficient farm infrastructure; and
- A shortage of young leaders in agriculture (see box, "Structural Change in Fruit Farming").

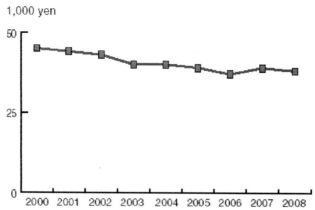

Source: Ministry of Internal Affairs and Communications, Family Income and Expenditure Survey.

Figure 1. Annual fruit expenditures per Japanese household (for at-home consumption)

Index, 2005=100

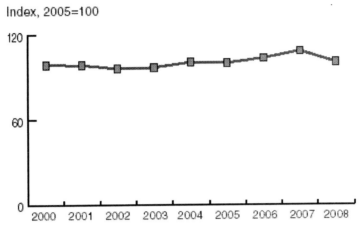

Note: CPI for fruits divided by CPI for all goods multiplied by 100. Source: ERS calculations based on Portal Site of Official Statistics of Japan, Statistics Bureau.

Figure 2. Fruit prices in Japan: Consumer price index (CPI) for fruits/consumer prices for all goods

Million U.S. dollars

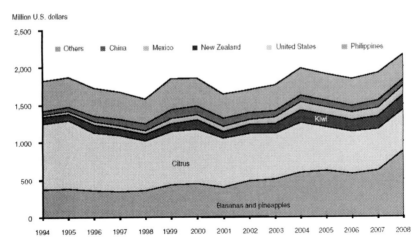

Note: Commodities with over $100 million import value from one country are listed in the originating country section.

Source: ERS calculations based on Japan trade statistics. Fruit categories included are those found in chapter 8 of the Harmonized System.

Figure 3. Japan's fruit imports, by country of origin

Table 2. Japan's Production and Imports of Fresh Fruit

Fruit crop	Japan's production, 2007	Import volume, 2008		Japan's tariff or tariff range
		From all sources	From the United States	
		Metric tons		*Percent*
Mandarin oranges/tangerines	1,066,000	10,228	7,780	17
Apples	840,100	37	0	17
Watermelons	421,600	99	61	6
Japanese pears	296,800	80	0	4.8
Persimmons	244,800	0	0	6
Other melons	221,300	31,073	6,612	6
Grapes	209,100	6,612	1,669	7.8-17
Strawberries	191,400	3,278	3,087	6
Peaches	150,200	0	0	6
Mume apricots	120,600	0	0	6
Kiwifruit	32,800	59,222	81	6.4
Other pears	29,600	0	0	4.8
Plums	21,900	0	0	6
Cherries	16,600	8,525	8,454	8.5
Pineapples	10,400	144,408	0	17
Oranges	9,000	97,818	71,486	16-32
Lemons and limes	5,250	59,357	36,728	0
Mangoes, guavas	2,300	11,589	285	0-3
Bananas	205	1,092,738	0	10-25
Grapefruit	0	184,022	126,097	10
Papaya	NA	3,817	889	0-2

Sources: ERS calculations based on Statistical Yearbook of the Ministry of Agriculture, Forestry and Fisheries, 2007-2008; USDA Production, Supply and Distribution database; United Nations, Food and Agriculture Organization, FAOSTAT; World Trade Atlas; table 4.

As in other countries, weather conditions affect Japan's fruit crops and sometimes create unbalanced supply-demand situations in the market. Therefore, market prices are fairly volatile and Japanese farmers often face unstable income prospects, especially if domestic demand is static. To address these issues, Government policies try to mitigate structural and market volatility in order to support and stabilize farmers' incomes.

Some Government policies help finance the adjustment to a larger-scale farm structure, and others regulate production, reduce risk, and support prices, with the goal of maintaining income. These policies include border protection. Some policies also aim to increase domestic demand. Changes to Japan's domestic fruit policies legislated in 2005 went into effect in 2007. The changes reflect the Japanese Government's intent to stimulate larger-scale agricultural production and yet to maintain relatively comprehensive support to all producers. These domestic regulations and subsidies, import taxes, and phytosanitary rules help define the Japanese market for imported fruit.

STRUCTURAL CHANGE IN FRUIT FARMING

Structural change in Japan's fruit farming industry has been slow. Since 1990, fruit area, output, and the number of farm households have all declined, with little indication that average farm size or per-hectare yield has increased (see figure below). Japan's topography and land ownership structure are not favorable to create large, unified farm operations. A thorough land reform after World War II helped keep Japan's farmland divided into millions of small holdings. These relatively small and scattered areas may be suitable for fruit production but would be quite expensive to consolidate by private owners. New policies encourage contract farming, renting out, cooperative farming, and other solutions that apply to all crops.

Japan's 2005 Census of Agriculture counted almost 300,000 farms that produced fruit in orchards, fields, or greenhouses, including many small-scale, part-time growers. In 2006, the last year with available data, 48,000 households growing fruit were classified as "business farms." This meant that the household received over 50 percent of its income from farming, that at least one family member spent 60 120 days or more on farm activities, and that the farmer was younger than 65 years.

Index: 1990=100

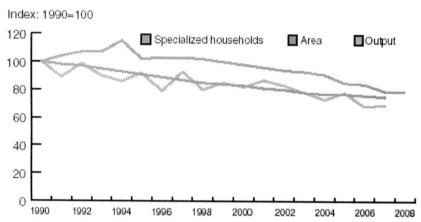

Note: Specialized households are those engaged just in fruit farming.
Source: ERS calculations based on data from the *Statistical Yearbook,* Ministry of
     Agriculture, Forestry and Fisheries.

Number of fruit farms, area, and output

The Government is eager to support the business farm and would like to see it proliferate by absorbing some of the part-time operations. This type of farm, however, has been decreasing in Japan, chiefly because farmers are aging beyond 65 years. In response, the Government continues to change its policy measures to encourage younger farmers to replace this aging population.

DOMESTIC POLICIES

Japan's domestic fruit policies are based on the 1961 Act on Special Measures Concerning the Promotion of Fruit-Growing Industries. Since then, the Ministry of Agriculture, Forestry and Fisheries (MAFF) has revised the Basic Policy for Fruit Industry Promotion (which implemented the 1961 Act) several times. In the most recent revision (spring 2005), Japan ended its existing policies supporting fruit markets and replaced them with a new set that went into effect on April 1, 2007.[4] Some of the new policies are similar to previous ones, and some are different. The 2005 Basic Policy looked at fruit production, farm management, distribution, exports, and consumption and suggested measures to revitalize Japan's fruit agriculture over a 10-year horizon.

The 2005 Basic Policy's key elements include:
- Reform of the fruit farming structure;
- The fostering of future agricultural leaders;
- Supply-demand adjustments;
- Management assistance and programs to help stabilize farm income; and
- Risk management tools (unchanged by the 2005 Basic Policy).

Japan's fruit-growing sector faces significant challenges, including insufficient farm labor, inefficient farm infrastructure, inflexible farmland usage, and other problems that lead to declining harvested areas and fruit production. In the 2005 Basic Policy, MAFF encourages the establishment of local farmers' committees to formulate a strategic plan for the next 5-10 years that focuses on structural reform to revitalize fruit-farming communities. The committees' plans should consider the viability of farming, future leadership, marketing, production, labor issues, and the like. MAFF strongly suggests that the plan should be developed by farmers.

Japan's policymakers and fruit farmers believe that the current structure of Japanese agriculture is unsustainable, because aging farmers are not likely to be replaced in equal measure by new farmers. The most recent policy changes (including the 2005 fruit policies) try to redirect Government funds toward farmers who are capable of expanding the size of their operations and who are adept at anticipating market changes and adjusting their output in response. Because previous policies subsidized all farmers, redirection of funds in 2007 means some farmers will get less funding than before.

On the demand side, the Basic Policy for Food, Agriculture and Rural Villages, which was issued by MAFF in March 2005, promoted consumption of locally grown fruits in the school lunch program and through farmers' markets.

Policy Measures Affecting Management, Supply and Demand, and Income

In April 2007, the Japanese Government put new measures into place for fruit farming and replaced the previous price-subsidy scheme with a new market stabilization program. These measures aim to stabilize farm businesses and farm income, in part, by improving farm structure in fruit producing

regions. The new fruit measures include two programs (effective from April 2007 to March 2011):
1. The Fruit Farm Management Support Program
2. The Fruit Supply-Demand Stabilization Program

The Fruit Farm Management Support Program

This program provides subsidies to farmers who transplant better fruit cultivars, improve farm infrastructure, hire labor, etc. The program applies to all fruit categories and has two tiers. The first tier helps farmers improve their production infrastructure, and the second helps agricultural producer cooperatives reform fruit production structures.

Subsidies are available to farmers for converting to better cultivars, grafting trees, or abandoning unproductive orchards/groves (table 3). Fruit farmers are also eligible to receive subsidies of up to half the total cost of infrastructure changes, such as improving farm roads, leveling hilly lands, improving the soil, and upgrading the waterways. These subsidies are only provided for two fruit crops: Mikan tangerines and apples. These fruits account for 60 percent of Japan's total fruit production. This program runs from April 1, 2007, to March 31, 2011, with a budget of 4.75 billion yen ($54.1 million) for each of the 4 years.

Table 3. Subsidies to Encourage Productivity and Structural Changes for Fruit Farming

Activity	Eligible fruit stock	Subsidy amount	
		Yen/10a[1]	U.S. dollars/acre[2]
Transplanting trees	Mikan tangerines	220,000	8,611
	Apples for dwarfing purposes	320,000	12,524
	Apples of regular cultivars	160,000	6,262
	Other fruit cultivars	Up to half the cost	
Grafting trees	All fruit cultivars	Up to half the cost	
Abandoning unproductive orchards or groves	Mikan tangerines	100,000	3,914
	Apples	80,000	3,131
	Other fruit trees	Up to half the cost	

[1] 10a (10 ares) are equal to 0.2471 acre.
[2] The average exchange rate was 103.4 yen per U.S. dollar in 2008.
Source: Ministry of Agriculture, Forestry and Fisheries of Japan (MAFF).

These subsidies help farmers expand, update, or abandon their orchards. The implicit intent is to encourage fruit farm restructuring, where younger, full- time farmers expand or update their production and older, smaller farmers exit the industry.

Subsidies are available to agricultural producers' cooperatives for production reform measures and cover up to half of the cost. Producer cooperatives are important in Japanese horticulture, as they set up collection, sorting, and packing facilities and arrange for marketing. Activities eligible for subsidy support include:

- Developing a reliable farm labor supply system;
- Developing an information system that supports farm leaders;
- Setting up large-scale seedling facilities;
- Supporting new technologies; and
- Supporting market development.

The Fruit Supply-Demand Stabilization Program

This program focuses on stabilizing market prices by adjusting production volumes and/or adjusting shipping volumes to the fresh market. It is similar to the Supply-Demand Adjustment Program that operated in 200 1-07 (see, "Appendix: Previous Fruit Policies"). Japan's Government notified the WTO that it spent 1.2 billion yen annually between 2001 and 2005 ($9.5-11 million U.S. dollars) on payments related to price, presumably for the Supply-Demand Adjustment Program.[5] Spending levels for the new program are not available. Currently, this program applies to only two major fruit crops: Mikan tangerines and apples. There are two tiers for this program: (1) the Planned Fruit Production project, and (2) the Emergency Supply-Demand Adjustment project.

The Planned Fruit Production Project

Each year, MAFF, local governments, and grower cooperatives set an adequate shipment volume for the season based on supply and demand projections and then inform local grower cooperatives so they can adjust their production to meet production targets. The production adjustment is usually carried out by culling fruit from trees early in the season (culled fruit is destroyed). Farmers who participate in this project are eligible for subsidies of half the cost incurred. Japan Agriculture (JA), the national farmers' cooperative, receives the funds from the national Government and passes it on to eligible producers.

The Emergency Supply-Demand Adjustment Project

At harvest, if Japan's total production exceeds an adequate market level, growers and grower cooperatives are asked to divert some product to the processing sector to avoid oversupply in the fresh market. Growers and grower cooperatives are eligible to receive 34 yen per kilogram (15 cents per pound) for fresh produce diverted to the processing market.

Risk Management

About 86,000 of Japan's fruit farms insured about 44,000 hectares in 2006 (the last year of available data).[6] One set of insurance policies applies to fruit and another to fruit trees or vines (after they have reached fruit-bearing age). Insurance for fruit can be comprehensive, covering yield decrease and/or quality deterioration caused by weather, fire, plant disease, insects, and other pests. Alternatively, a farmer can insure only against damage from storm, hail, or frost. Farmers can choose to insure yields for the entire farm or on a plot-by-plot basis. Yield and quality are both insured if a farmer chooses to insure a standard income level. Tree/vine insurance covers plant death or heavy damage if trees wither, are washed away, disappear, or are buried.

Insurance programs are available for the following fruits :[7]

- All citrus fruits;
- Apples, pears, peaches, cherries, Japanese apricots, and plums;
- Grapes and kiwis;
- Persimmons, chestnuts, loquats, and pineapples.

Japan's agricultural insurance is centrally organized and was not changed by the 2005 Basic Policy. Agricultural Mutual Relief (AMR) associations are locally based and act as the primary insurance agents for farm activities. They collect premiums and dispense indemnities when claims are made. The AMR associations are grouped into prefectural AMR associations, which act as reinsurers for the local AMRs.[8] MAFF acts as the reinsurer for the prefectural AMRs and pays half the insurance premium for fruit farmers as a subsidy. MAFF also pays part of the administrative costs for the local and prefectural

AMRs (National Agricultural Insurance Association (NAIA), 2005). In 2007, MAFF paid premiums of 2.2 billion yen ($19 million) for fruit farmers (NAIA, 2009).

The premium rate is estimated every 3 years and primarily depends on the farm damage rate over the previous 20 years. The Government matches the amount paid by farmers. In 2004, the average participating fruit farmer paid 33,000 yen for about 0.5 hectare of fruit area (i.e., about $305 for 1.19 acres).

Indemnities for ordinary damage, such as setbacks for an individual farm, are paid jointly by the local and prefectural AMR associations. For extensive damage (e.g., damage over a wide area), most of the indemnity is paid by the national Government, with 20 percent of the indemnity coming from the local and prefectural AMR associations (NAIA, 2005). In 2006, indemnities of 4.858 billion yen ($42 million) were paid out for damaged fruit and trees. In recent years, aggregate premium revenue has been larger than indemnities.[9]

In addition to the insurance program, the Japan Finance Corporation (a Government corporation) offers low-interest loans (current rate for the loans is 1.10-1.25 percent annually) to cover costs when farm operations are damaged by acts of nature, such as typhoons, heavy rainfall, drought, cold weather, or earthquake.[10]

School Lunch and Other Consumption Programs

MAFF promotes "local production for local consumption" (*chisan chisho*) to improve Japan's food self-sufficiency so that it is in line with the Basic Policy for Food, Agriculture and Rural Villages (March 2005). The school lunch program and farmers' markets help promote local production and consumption.

The Basic Policy for Dietary Education Promotion (March 2006) states that school lunch programs should supply over 30 percent of their foodstuff with locally produced products by 2010 (as a national average). The policy promotes locally produced products for local consumption to build trust between growers and consumers and also to improve public interest in and understanding of fresh local foods. The definition of "local production for local consumption" is food produced and consumed within the same prefecture. In 2006, about 21 percent of school lunch consumption was provided by local production. A survey in 2004 found that 76.6 percent of schools used "local production for local consumption" food in their school lunch programs, while only 14 percent of schools did not use any locally produced products.

Food demand for Japan's school lunch program is estimated at approximately 500 billion yen ($5 billion) annually. There are no Government subsidies for fruit purchases by school lunch programs.[11]

Japan's school lunch program uses relatively few imported fruits. Imported grapefruit, oranges, bananas, and kiwifruit are served for dessert in school lunches when domestic fruit supply is down. Dried-fruit products, such as California prunes and raisins, are occasionally served in school lunches.

There are approximately 13,000 farmers' markets throughout Japan. About 3,000 markets are operated by agricultural cooperatives or local governments. Average annual sales per market are approximately 60 million yen ($580,000) at markets operated by cooperatives or local governments.

Farmers' markets are often found in local Government parking lots or in a local shopping mall on weekends. Some large-scale farmers' markets are permanently established roadside on major highways. Farmers pick seasonal fruits and vegetables early in the morning and display them at a nearby farmers' market on the same day so that consumers can buy fresh-picked products at a reasonable price.

Two major nonprofit organizations are also active in consumption programs for fresh vegetables and fruits in Japan. The Five-a-Day Association promotes fruit and vegetable consumption through dietary education—"Let's eat five servings of vegetables (350 grams) and two servings of fruit (200 grams) every day." The organization consists of over 130 companies, including supermarkets, trading companies, food processing companies, and growers.[12] Activities for Vegefru-seven are similar to those of the Five-a-Day program and promote fruit and vegetable consumption through dietary education and encouragement of a healthy lifestyle.[13]

BORDER POLICIES

The import of fresh fruits and fruit products into Japan must overcome a number of obstacles—tariffs and sanitary standards—that ultimately affect cost and product availability. Fruit tariffs are set ad valorem (according to the product's value) and may vary according to the source country, the season, and the form (fresh or processed) of the fruit. In addition to the tariffs, fruit imports must meet phytosanitary and sanitary standards. In many cases, these standards are greater barriers to imports than the tariffs.

Table 4. Japan's Tariffs on Fruit Imports by Exporting Countries' Development Level

| Fruit | Fresh | | | | | |
| | Full year or in-season | | | Out-of-season | | |
	Developed	Developing	Least-developed	Developed	Developing	Least-developed
			Percent			
Bananas	25	20	0	20	10	0
Dates	0					
Figs	6	3	0			
Pineapples	17	17	0			
Avocados	3	0	0			
Guavas and mangoes	3	0	0			
Durians, rambutan, passionfruit, etc.	5	2.5	0			
Pawpaws/ papayas	2	0	0			
Oranges	32	32	0	16	16	0
Mandarins/ tangerines	17	17	0			
Lemons and limes	0					
Grapefruit	10	10	0	10	10	0
Grapes	17	17	0	7.8	7.8	0
Melons	6	6	0			
Apples	17	17	0			
Pears	4.8	4.8	0			
Apricots	6	6	0			
Cherries	8.5	8.5	0			
Peaches	6	6	0			
Plums	6	6	0			
Persimmons	6	6	0			
Strawberries	6	6	0			
Cranberries	6	3	0			
Other berries	6	3	0			
Kiwi	6.4	6.4	0			
Bananas[1]	12	12	0	25/20	25/20	0	3	0	0
Dates	12	12	0	12	12	0	0		
Figs	12	12	0	12	12	0	6	3	0
Pineapples	23.8	23.8	0	12	12	0	7.2	7.2	0

Table 4. (Continued)

Fruit	Fresh								
	Full year or in-season			Out-of-season					
	Developed	Developing	Least-developed	Developed	Developing	Least-developed	Developed	Developing	Least-developed
Avocados[2]	12/7.2	12/3.6	0	12	10	0	3	0	0
Guavas and mangoes[2]	12/7.2	12/3.6	0	12	10	0	3	0	0
Durians, rambutan, passionfruit, etc.[2]	12/7.2	12/3.6	0	12	6	0	7.5	3.8	0
Pawpaws/papayas[2]	12/7.2	6/3.6	0	12	6	0	7.5	3.8	0
Oranges[1]	12	12	0	32/16	32/16	0	32/16	32/16	0
Mandarins/tangerines	12	12	0	17	17	0	17	17	0
Lemons/limes	12	12	0	0		0			
Grapefruit	12	12	0	10	10	0	10	10	0
Grapes	12	12	0	12	12	0	1.2	0	0
Melons	12	12	0	12	12	0	9	9	0
Apples	12	12	0	12	12	0	9	9	0
Pears	7	7	0	12	12	0	9	9	0
Apricots	12	12	0	12	12	0	9	9	0
Cherries[3]	13.8	6.9	0	17	17	0	9	9	0
Peaches	7	7	0	12	12	0	9	9	0
Plums	12	12	0	12	12	0	2.4	0	0
Persimmons	12	12	0	12	12	0	9	9	0
Strawberries[2]	9.6/12	9.6/12	0	12	12	0	9	9	0
Cranberries	12	12	0	12	12	0	9	9	0
Other berries[2]	9.6/6	4.8/3	0	12	12	0	9	9	0
Kiwi	12	12	0	12	12	0	9	9	0

Notes: This should not be regarded as an authoritative or complete listing. For more information, check the Customs Tariff Schedules of Japan.

[1] Seasonal tariffs apply to provisionally preserved and/or dried fruit, indicated by two tariffs separated by a "/".

[2] Tariffs differ in one or more processed categories, depending on whether sugar has been added. The first tariff refers to product with sugar added, and the second to product without added sugar. Tariffs are separated by "/".

[3] Tariffs in the frozen category are for sour cherries containing added sugar. The tariff on other cherries is 12 percent for developed and developing countries.

Source: Customs Tariff Schedules of Japan, 2008.

Tariffs

Japan's tariffs on fruit range from 0 to 32 percent of the value (table 4). The highest tariff—32 percent—applies to oranges imported between December and May, when Japan's main citrus crop is marketed.[14] For all fruit—fresh, dried, frozen, or provisionally preserved[15]—the tariff for least-developed countries is zero.[16] For many developing countries, the tariff is less than that for developed countries.[17] Tariffs on imports from developed countries are generally more than zero, except for fresh dates, lemons, and limes, which face no tariff.

Tariffs also vary depending on whether a fruit is imported in fresh, frozen, dried, or provisionally preserved form. Tariffs on frozen[18] and provisionally preserved[19] fruits are typically 12 percent for imports from developed countries, while tariffs on dried fruits are often 9 percent.[20] Thus, in general, tariffs are highest on frozen and provisionally preserved fruit imports (presumably to protect Japanese fruit processors) and on fresh oranges, bananas, pineapples, mikan tangerines, and grapes—all fruits with some production in Japan.

Phytosanitary Rules

Japan prohibits fruit imports from many parts of the world (Korea is the main exception) due to 17 pests that may be found in or on the product.[21] Two— codling moth and fire blight—are significant for temperate fruits. Some countries—notably the United States, Australia, New Zealand, and Chile—have negotiated exceptions to trade bans on some fruits (table 5, for U.S. fruits).[22] Japan permits imports of apples, cherries, plums, and nectarines from the United States if "shipped directly, meeting standards of MAFF."23,[24] U.S. apricots and peaches, among other fruits, are not allowed entry because of codling moth concerns, and U.S. pears are barred because of both codling moth and fire blight.

Japan's Plant Protection Station is a MAFF agency that regulates plant disease issues both for domestic and imported items. It inspects shipments at Japanese ports and can accept or reject them. It also inspects plant protection systems in exporting countries for their treatments of certain pests.

Table 5. Quarantine Conditions for Various U.S. Fruits

Fresh fruit	Cultivars	Year market opened	Pest	Required treatment
Papaya[1]	Solo	1969	Mediterranean fruit fly, Oriental fruit fly complex, and melon fly	Vapor heat treatment
Mango[1]	Keitt	2000		
	Haden			
Cherry	Bing	1978	Codling moth	Methyl bromide fumigation
	Lambert			
	Van	1986		
	Rainier	1992		
	Garnet	1995		
	Tulare	1996		
	Brooks			
	Lapin	1999		
	Sweet Heart			
	Chelan	2001		
	All other cherry cultivars	2001		
Walnuts (in shell)	Hartley	1986	Codling moth	Methyl bromide fumigation
	Payne			
	Franquette			
Nectarine	Summer Grand	1988	Codling moth	Methyl bromide fumigation
	Spring Red			
	Fir Ebrite			
	Fantasia			
	May Grand			
	Red Diamond			
	May Fine	1993		.
	May Glo			
	May Diamond			
	Royal Giant	1995		
	All other nectarines	2000		
European plum	D'agen	2001	Codling moth	Methyl bromide fumigation
	Tulare Giant	2005		
	Moyer			
	All other European plums			

Table 5. (Continued)

Fresh fruit	Cultivars	Year market opened	Pest	Required treatment
Apple[2]	Red Delicious	1994	Codling moth	Cold treatment
	Golden Delicious		Fire blight	Methyl bromide fumigation
	Fuji	1999		
	Braeburn			
	Granny Smith			
	Gala			
	Jona Gold			
	All other apples	2001		

[1] Hawaiian Islands only.

[2] Washington, Oregon, and California only.

Source: Japan Fresh Produce Import and Safety Association.

Nearly 60 percent of U.S. grapefruit exports to Japan were fumigated at the port of entry in 2008 (table 6), as were significant shares of oro blanco, raspberry, and lemons. Rejections of fruit were much less common.

The United States' ability to export apples, cherries, plums, and nectarines has involved protracted negotiations with Japan. From 1994 to 2005, apples grown for Japanese markets could only come from certain U.S. growing areas and from specific parts of orchards separated by 10-meter buffers from trees bearing apples not designated for Japanese markets. Orchard inspections by MAFF officials at the small fruit stage, chlorine dips, fumigation, and post-harvest inspection all added to the cost of producing such apples. Negotiations with the United States and other trading partners, followed by a WTO case which Japan lost, led to the adoption of a less restrictive, but still onerous, system in August 2005 that includes:

- 55 days of cold treatment;
- Methyl-bromide fumigation; and
- Intensive inspections by MAFF officers.[25]

In 2009, Japan revised its phytosanitary restrictions on U.S. cherries to allow imports without methyl-bromide fumigation if three conditions are met:

1. Imported crop must come from fields that have had few cases of codling moths;
2. Inspections must take place before the crops are exported from the United States and then again when they arrive in Japan, and;
3. Japanese quarantine officials must periodically carry out onsite inspections of U.S. orchards.[26]

Table 6. Fresh Fruit Plant Quarantine Inspection Results: Imports from the United States, 2008

Fruit	Inspected (kg)	Fumigated at entry to Japan (kg)	Rejected (kg)	Percent fumigated[1]	Percent rejected[2]
Lemons	36,734,426	2,912,390	34	7.9	0.00
Grapefruit	122,924,745	78,498,271	22,450	63.9	0.02
Oranges	71,801,074	1,140,082	4	1.6	0.00
Minneolas	7,460,168	141,303	0	1.9	0.00
Oro blancos	1,412,145	108,814	0	7.7	0.00
Avocados	138,194	0	0	0.0	0.00
Mangos	287,244	0	1	0.0	0.00
Papaya	926,530	0	21	0.0	0.00
Kiwifruit	84,651	0	0	0.0	0.00
Cherry	8,472,838	0	11,364	0.0	0.13
Raspberry	427,446	23,678	0	5.5	0.00
Table grapes	1,923,643	101,483	282	5.3	0.01
Pomegranates	274,174	10,866	0	4.0	0.00

[1] Fumigated volume as percent of the total volume inspected. Products were fumigated at the port of entry, then imported into Japan.

[2] Rejected volume as percent of the total volume inspected. Products were denied entry into Japan.

Notes: Using lemons as an example, 36,734,426 kilograms of U.S. lemons were inspected and 2,912,390 kilograms (7.9 percent of the total imports) were ordered to be fumigated at the port of entry in 2008; 34 kg were rejected for entry into Japan.

Source: Ministry of Agriculture, Forestry and Fisheries of Japan (MAFF), 2009. Plant Quarantine Statistics (compiled by FAS/Tokyo).

As a result of these new phytosanitary restrictions, U.S. exporters can send cherries by ship instead of by air. Without fumigation, the cherries have a longer shelf life, allowing for ocean shipment that is less expensive than air freight.[27] Similar changes were made for plums and nectarines, but trade has yet to occur.

POLICY IMPLICATIONS

Japan's Supply-Demand Stabilization Program aims to keep prices stable and at a relatively high level. Because phytosanitary and tariff barriers often keep imports out, controlling domestic supplies may help maintain market prices. Consumers may pay a higher price in most years as a result of this policy, however, and may consume less fruit than if supply were unfettered and prices were lower. Government efforts to restructure fruit farming into larger, more efficient units could lead to lower-cost production, and, potentially, to lower market prices. Structural change, however, has been modest to date.

Japan's fruit prices are often higher than those of neighboring countries and those in the United States. Since the quality of fruits marketed in Japan is very high, the higher prices may be a quality premium. Branding fresh fruits is reportedly more prevalent in Japan than in the United States, and may allow some premiums to be added to market prices.[28] Border measures imposed by Japan's Government, however, are another price factor. Otherwise, high-quality fruits could be imported relatively soon after picking from countries where prices are much lower. Japan's tariffs on oranges and other fruits may impede some trade, but tariffs on many fruits are relatively low.[29] Phytosanitary rules also affect fruit trade by preventing some imports, raising the cost of others, and/or degrading the fruit.

The Organisation for Economic Co-operation and Development (OECD) estimated that consumers paid 63 billion yen ($609 million) more for grapes, 49.74 billion yen ($481 million) more for pears, 20.2 billion yen ($195 million) more for apples, and 10 billion yen ($93 million) more for strawberries in 2008 than if they had purchased them at an international reference price.[30]

At the farmgate, a comparison of Japanese producer prices and U.S. free-onboard (fob) shipping-point prices for seven fruits shows that Japan's farmers receive prices 1.5 to 7.5 times higher than those realized by U.S. farmers (figure 4). The highest price ratios in 20 04-07 were for watermelons, peaches, strawberries, and pears. The lowest price ratios were for grapes. At the retail level, price ratios in 2004-08 for six comparable fruits ranged from 1.2 to almost 3 times higher in Japan than in the United States (figure 5). Such comparisons, whether at the farmgate or retail, cannot account for quality differences, which can be considerable.

Lemons, which enter Japan without tariff, offer a useful point of reference. In 2006, lemon prices in Tokyo ranged from a low of 1.34 times the average price in U.S. urban areas to a high of 1.68 times the U.S. price. Because neither country imposes significant border tariffs, comparing lemon prices may demonstrate how market conditions, rather than Government policies, affect fruit prices.[31] In this comparison, Tokyo's retail prices appear to be roughly 50 percent higher than U.S. urban prices. Bananas are also imported by both countries. Japan imposes tariffs of 10 or 20 percent (depending on the season) on banana imports from principal exporting countries,[32] and Tokyo's retail prices are 1.75-2 times higher than U.S. urban prices. This price difference does not reflect higher production prices.[33] Rather, the price reflects the tariff as well as marketing and transport charges unique to Japan.[34]

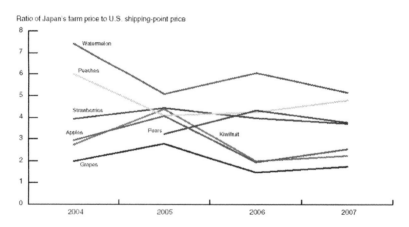

Sources: ERS calculations based on Ministry of Agriculture, Forestry and Fisheries of Japan (MAFF) monthly statistics and data from Lucier (2008) and Perez and Pollack (2008).

Figure 4. Japan-U.S. producer fruit price ratio

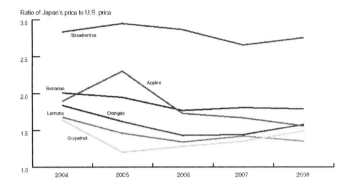

Sources: ERS calculations based on Ministry of Agriculture, Forestry and Fisheries of Japan (MAFF) monthly statistics and data from Perez and Pollack (2008).

Figure 5. Japan-U.S. retail fruit price ratio

The highest price ratio in the available set of comparable retail prices is for strawberries. Tokyo's retail strawberry prices are 2.65-2.95 times higher for strawberries than in the United States. Producer prices in Japan are 3.5-4.5 times higher than in the United States. Strawberries are a relatively perishable crop, which likely raises transport costs. Tariffs on fresh strawberries are relatively low (6 percent for strawberries from the United States and all countries geographically close to Japan), but phytosanitary rules may be an obstacle—Japan reports no imports from China, a large, nearby producing country.[35]

Farmers in exporting countries could increase exports if Japan's fruit market were more accessible. Table 2 shows a generally inverse relationship between fruit production and imports: Imports are relatively minor for the fruits Japan produces the most of, and domestic production is minor for fruits which Japan imports the most. However, varietal differences, seasonal differences, and price factors can lead to trade even when a country produces a great volume of a fruit. For example, Japan imports significant amounts of tangerines, melons, grapes, and strawberries, despite large domestic production. Trade is negligible or nonexistent for a number of fruits—pears, persimmons, peaches, apricots, and plums—with tariffs of 6 percent or less (see table 2). Trade in these markets is likely discouraged by phytosanitary regulations.

In general, even though the relatively high tariffs on oranges, apples, grapes, and pineapples hinder imports of these fruits, perhaps the greatest opportunity to improve imports in Japan could come by addressing phytosanitary issues. Fumigation, for example, affects fruit quality. Alternative phytosanitary rules would allow imports to be priced lower, and also increase imports of the fruit cultivars grown in the rest of the world but currently unavailable in Japan.

CONCLUSIONS

Japan's trade policies were created to support fruit production, and generous subsidies help farmers improve their orchards. The Government protects farmers against natural hazards (damage and disease) with insurance subsidies. Protection against market risk (chiefly lower prices) is achieved by culling fruit or through subsidies to farmers who send some fruit to processing rather than to fresh markets. Subsidies also help farmers exit the sector, encouraging farm consolidation. Despite this financial support, structural change has been slow, and the fruit farm sector has gradually shrunk while the average age of fruit farmers has risen.

Consumers in Japan pay higher fruit prices because of internal supply-management policies, tariffs, and phytosanitary rules applied to imports. To some extent, consumers may also pay higher prices because of real or perceived quality differences, branding efforts, or higher marketing costs. Given lower prices, consumers could save money but would also be likely to purchase more fruit.[36] Consumers (taxpayers) also pay as their tax dollars fund supply-management, hazard insurance, orchard improvement, and infra-structural support subsidies provided to fruit farmers.

At the Japanese border, relatively high tariffs apply to some fruit imports. Phytosanitary regulations, however, constitute the main impediment to imports, especially regulations that target codling moths and fire blight. Of the 19 major fruits produced in Japan, 8 fruit crops see no import activity, likely as a result of phytosanitary barriers. U.S. fruit producers, who currently export almost $500 million in fruit products to Japan, would benefit if Japan reduced its tariffs and if they could consistently meet Japan's phytosanitary standards, either by improving U.S. management and technology or by revising Japan's strict standards. Japan's consumers would also benefit from lower prices stemming from increased import supply.

REFERENCES

[1]   California Cherry Advisory Board. (2009). *Export Manual.*
[2]   Calvin, Linda & Barry Krissoff. (2005). *Resolution of the U.S.-Japan Apple Dispute; New Opportunities for Trade,* U.S. Department of Agriculture, Economic Research Service, Outlook Report FTS-318-01, October, http://www.ers.usda.gov/publications/FTS/Oct05/fts31801/.
[3]   Fukuda, Hisao, John Dyck & Jim Stout. (2003). *Rice Sector Policies in Japan,* U.S. Department of Agriculture, Economic Research Service, Outlook Report RCS 0303-01, March, *http://www.ers.usda.gov/ publications/rcs/ mar03/rcs03030 1/.*
[4]   Japan Fresh Produce Import & Safety Association. (2008). *Yearbook,* 2008. Japan Tariff Association. *Customs Tariff Schedules of Japan.*
[5]   Lucier, Gary. (2008). *Vegetables and Melons Situation and Outlook Yearbook,* VGS-2008, U.S. Department of Agriculture, Economic Research Service, May, *http://www.ers.usda.gov/publications/ VGS/ index.* htm#yearbook.
[6]   Ministry of Agriculture, Forestry & Fisheries (MAFF) [Japan]. 2007-(2008). *Monthly Statistics of Agriculture, Forestry and Fisheries,* various issues.
[7]   *Statistical Yearbook of Agriculture, Forestry and Fisheries.*
[8]   "New Fruit Measures—Farm Management Supports for Fruit Production," http://www:maff.go.jp/work/newfruits.pdf.
[9]   "The Basic Policy for the Fruit Industry Promotion," http://www. maff.go.jp/www/press/cont2/20050330press_8b.pdf.
[10] "Quick Understanding! New Fruit Industry Measures (Fruit Industry Management Support / Supply-Demand Stabilization Measures)," http:// www.maff.go.jp/j/seisan/engei/fruits
[11] "The Expansion of the Use of Locally Produced Agricultural Products to School Lunch Programs," http://www.maff.go.jp/j/seisan/gijutu/ tisan_tisyo/pdf/kyushoku.pdf.
[12] *"The Promotion of the Local Production for Local Consumption at Farm Stands,"* http://www.maff.go.jp/chisanchisyo/pdf/pamph.pdf.
[13] Interviews by Kenzo Ito with MAFF staff via phone conference.
[14] Ministry of Internal Affairs and Communication [Japan], Statistics Bureau. *Family Income and Expenditure Survey,* http://www.e-stat.go.jp/SG1/estat/ ListE.do?lid=00000 1055 113.

[15] Mori, Hiroshi, John Dyck, Susan Pollack, and Kimiko Ishibashi. *The Japa-nese Market for Oranges,* U.S. Department of Agriculture, Economic

[16] Research Service, FTS-330-01, March 2008, http://www.ers.usda.gov/ Publications/FTS/2008/03Mar/FTS3300 1/FTS3300 1 .pdf.

[17] Mori, Hiroshi, Dennis Clason, Kimiko Ishibashi, William D. Gorman & John Dyck. (2009). *Declining Orange Consumption in Japan: Generational Changes, Or Something Else?* ERR-71, U.S. Department of Agriculture, Economic Research Service, February, http://www.ers.usda.gov/ Publications/ERR7 1/

[18] National Agricultural Insurance Association. (2005). *The Outline of Japan's Agricultural Insurance Scheme,* printed brief, Japan.

[19] National Agricultural Insurance Association. (2009). *The Outline of Japan's Agricultural Insurance Scheme,* printed brief, Japan.

[20] Organisation for Economic Co-operation and Development. (2010). *Producer and Consumer Support Estimates,* OECD Data-base 1986-2008, *http://www.oecd.org/document/59/0,3343*,en_2649_33797_3955 1355_1_1_1_37401,00.html

[21] Perez, Agnes & Susan Pollack. (2008). *Fruit and Tree Nuts Yearbook,* FTS-2008, U.S. Department of Agriculture, Economic Research Service, October, http://www.ers.usda.gov/publications/FTS/index.htm#yearbook.

[22] U.S. Department of Agriculture, Foreign Agricultural Service, Tokyo. *Daily Agricultural Highlights,* various issues.

APPENDIX: PREVIOUS FRUIT POLICIES

The old fruit policies focused on adjusting supply-demand to stabilize market prices and on stabilizing farm management through farm income support. These old measures were in effect from 2001 to April 2007, when they were replaced by the new fruit import and production policies.

Supply-Demand Adjustment Project

This project was effective from April 2001 to March 2007 and applied to mikan tangerines and apples. Each year, MAFF set production and shipment levels by looking at supply and demand situations and then prompted local JA's (agricultural growers' cooperatives) to adjust their production plans (often through culling) to meet goals for the season (app. table 1).

Management Stabilization Project

If market prices fell below a predetermined standard price, growers participating in the Supply-Demand Adjustment Project were eligible for price subsidies. This price subsidy program ended in March 2007 and enabled growers to receive a direct payment equal to approximately 80 percent of the difference between the actual market price and the predetermined standard price for subsidies, per unit of output. Fifty percent of the fund that provided the subsidies was contributed by MAFF and the rest by local governments and participating member growers.[37] The standard price for subsidies was determined by an average market price for the last 6 years adjusted with each year's variation coefficient. The standard price was established for each prefecture for each season. For the first 4 years of the project (200 1-04), the total amount of subsidies paid out was 18.8 billion yen ($160 million, at the 2008 yen/dollar exchange rate) to unshu mikan growers and 7.2 billion yen ($61 million) to apple growers (app. table 2). Subsidy amounts for each prefecture varied by fruit crop based on average market prices and the standard price for subsidies in 2005 (app. table 3).

Rice Diversion Payments

Under the rice diversion program (ended in 2007), farmers were encouraged to plant fruit orchards in former rice paddies, addressing two issues:

1. Reducing rice production, which exceeded demand; and,
2. Increasing fruit production, which the Government favored.

In 2001, for example, the annual rice diversion payment was as high as 150,000 yen/hectare ($1,240 U.S. dollars).[38]

Appendix Table 1. Supply-Demand Target and Actual Levels, 2004-2005

Levels	Mikan tangerines		Apples	
	Production	Shipment	Production	Shipment
2004	Metric tons			
Actual levels (a)	1,060,000	937,000	754,000	667,000
Target levels (b)	1,110,000	985,000	870,000	780,000
Ratio (a/b)	96%	95%	87%	86%
2005				
Actual levels (a)	1,130,000	1,010,000	819,000	724,000
Target levels (b)	1,110,000	985,000	870,000	780,000
Ratio (a/b)	102%	102%	94%	93%

Source: Ministry of Agriculture, Forestry and Fisheries

Appendix Table 2. Management Stabilization Subsidies

Year	Mikan tangerines	Apples	Total
	Billion yen		
2001	11.8	3.3	15.1
2002	3.4	3.9	7.3
2003	3.6	0	3.6
2004	0.3	0	0.3
Sum	18.8	7.2	26.0

Note: Totals may not sum due to rounding.
Source: Ministry of Agriculture, Forestry and Fisheries.

Appendix Table 3. Mikan Tangerines: Major Prefectures

Prefecture	Average price(March 2006)	Standard price for subsidy	Subsidy amount paid	Average per-farm subsidy paid
	Yen/kg	Yen/kg	Billion yen	Thousand yen
Shizuoka	173	185	0.8	141
Wakayama	149	160	0.8	126
Hiroshima	110	145	0.8	191
Ehime	155	170	0.5	69
Fukuoka	130	140	0.1	106
Saga	127	140	0.4	122
Nagasaki	147	150	0.1	26
Kumamoto	124	150	1.3	517

Notes: Seventeen prefectures participated in the program and received subsidies. Total subsidies paid were 5.1 billion yen in 2005. The average exchange rate was 110.2 yen per U.S. dollar in 2005.
Source: Ministry of Agriculture, Forestry and Fisheries.

End Notes

[1] 1.193 trillion yen, from *Statistical Yearbook* of the Ministry of Agriculture, Forestry and Fisheries, 2007-08, p. 550.

[2] U.S. exports of fruits and fruit preparations, not including fruit juice.

[3] Weather-related problems in North America (oranges and lemons) and low yields in Japan (mikan tangerines, persimmons, peaches, and others) reduced supplies and pushed prices higher in 2007.

[4] The old policies included an income stabilization program related to farm- gate prices for fruit; national supply- demand management to prevent prices from falling below desired levels; and payments to plant orchards in diverted rice paddies. These policies are described briefly in "Appendix: Previous Fruit Policies."

[5] Notifications G/AG/N/JPN 108, 124, 129, and 132, accessible at *http:// docsonline.wto.org/ gen_search.* asp?searchmode=advanced. In these notifications, Japan exempted the payments from the Aggregate Measurement of Support because they constituted only 0.2 percent of the farm value of production, and thus fell under the de minimis rule of the WTO's Agreement on Agriculture.

[6] *Statistical Yearbook* of the Ministry of Agriculture, Forestry and Fisheries, 2007-08, p. 670. The growing area for major fruits was about 225,000 hectares in 2006. Thus, about 20 percent was insured.

[7] No insurance is provided for strawberries or other fruits not listed, unless they are grown in greenhouses. A separate insurance program covers greenhouse crops.

[8] Japan is divided into approximately 50 prefectures, which are regional governments with significant capacity to encourage and regulate agriculture within their boundaries.

[9] *Statistical Yearbook* of the Ministry of Agriculture, Forestry and Fisheries, 2007-08, p. 671.

[10] Created in 2008, Japan Finance Corporation (*http://www.jfc.go.jp/*) consolidated four finance corporations: the Public Finance Corporation; the Agriculture, Forestry and Fisheries Finance Corporation; the Japan Finance Corporation for Small Business; and the Japan Bank for International Cooperation.

[11] In 1978-2000, mikan juice was subsidized by 2-5 yen/kg. The program ended in 2000.

[12] http://www.5aday.net/

[13] http://www.vf7.jp/

[14] Mori et al. provide more information about Japan's orange tariff and the seasonal pattern of orange trade.

[15] Provisionally preserved fruits are cooked, dried, or otherwise changed so that they can be easily shipped to processing facilities for inclusion in finished consumer food items.

[16] Least-developed countries in Asia include Burma, Cambodia, Laos, the Maldives, Bangladesh, East Timor, Afghanistan, Nepal, Bhutan, and Yemen. Least-developed countries outside Asia include Haiti, many countries in Africa, and certain island countries in Oceania.

[17] Developing countries in Asia include China and all countries and territories in Asia except 1) those in the least-developed group (see footnote 16) and 2) North Korea, Taiwan, Hong Kong, Singapore, Macao, Brunei, Bahrain, Kuwait, Qatar, Oman, Israel, and the United Arab Emirates. North Korea faces statutory tariffs that are generally higher than those faced by developed countries.

[18] Tariffs on frozen sour cherries and frozen pineapples are higher at 13.8 percent and 23.8 percent, respectively.

[19] Tariffs on provisionally preserved bananas, oranges, mikan tangerines, and cherries are higher than 12 percent.

[20] Only tariffs on dried oranges and tangerines are higher than 9 percent.

[21] See MAFF, "List of the plants which are prohibited to be imported (Plant Protection Law Enforcement Regulations Annexed Table 2)" at http://www. pps.go.jp/english/law/list2-(080911-). html.

[22] Calvin and Krissoff (2005) provide an overview, p. 5.

[23] "These standards include the terms and conditions for the type and variety of plants, its production area, methods of sterilization, means of transportation, etc." See http://www.pps.go.jp/english/ jobs/index.html.

[24] Calvin and Krissoff review the history of Japan's phytosanitary controls on cherry imports (p. 4).

[25] Calvin and Krissoff (2005) provide more detail and discussion of the effects of the new protocol (pp. 11-12).

[26] FAS/Tokyo, Daily Agricultural Highlights, March 31 and July 2, 2009; and California Cherry Advisory Board, 2009 Export Manual.

[27] Associated Press, Shannon Dininny, "New inspection rules help Western cherry exporters," *FA S/Tokyo Daily Agricultural Highlights,* July 9, 2009.

[28] Based on a review by William Gorman and Hiroshi Mori, November 14, 2009.

[29] Mori et al. (2009) estimated an own- price elasticity of -1.3 for oranges purchased for home use in Japan. Because the tariff raises the price of oranges in Japan, price-sensitive consumers may purchase fewer oranges because of the tariff.

[30] Organisation for Economic Cooperation and Development (OECD), Producer and Consumer Support Estimates, OECD Database 1986-2008, accessed 2/3/10.

[31] Transportation charges to the importing country may also differ.

[32] Japan's tariffs are designed to support its small banana production on southern islands, such as Okinawa.

[33] Japan imports mostly from the Philippines, while the United States is supplied principally by Central and South America. Free-on-board export unit values in the exporting countries are similar, regardless of whether the trade flow is to Japan or to the United States.

[34] MAFF conducted a survey of retail prices in November 2006, finding that retail prices were lower in New York City for bananas (87 percent of those in Tokyo); and that grapefruits and apples were more expensive in New York City than in Tokyo (127 percent and 110 percent, respectively). *Statistical Yearbook* of the Ministry of Agriculture, Forestry and Fisheries, 2007-08, p. 685. Prices in New York City tend to be higher than in the rest of the United States.

[35] Official Japanese trade data, reported by the World Trade Atlas.

[36] Calvin and Krissoff (2005) estimate consumer impacts of Japan's phytosanitary controls on apples.

[37] Nineteen prefectures participated annually in the case of unshu mikan tangerines and six in the case of apples.

[38] Fukuda, Dyck, and Stout, pp. 7-8

In: Fruit in Japan: Policies and Issues   ISBN: 978-1-61761-115-5
Editors: Paul C. Bradley   © 2010 Nova Science Publishers, Inc.

Chapter 2

THE JAPANESE MARKET FOR ORANGES

United States Department of Agriculture

STRACT

Japan is a large market for U.S. oranges, and most of Japan's orange consumption is supplied by U.S. exports. Orange consumption and imports grew until 1994, but have declined since. Demographic shifts are linked to changing orange consumption: older birth cohorts eat more oranges, and younger ones eat fewer oranges; within each cohort, consumption increases with age. Income changes appear not to be major factors in the decline in orange consumption, but price changes appear to be potentially important. A downward trend in consumption, not explained by the demographic variables, prices, or income, may continue in the future.

ACKNOWLEDGMENTS

The authors gratefully acknowledge the reviews of Agnes Perez, Sophia Huang, Mary Anne Normile, Daniel Pick, Noel Gollehon, William Coyle, and Janet Perry of USDA's Economic Research Service; Kenzo Ito of USDA's Foreign Agricultural Service; John Love of USDA's World Agricultural Outlook Board; and an anonymous reviewer. Excellent support was provided by the editor, Dale Simms, and by the designer, Cynthia Ray.

Keywords: Japan, oranges, citrus, age/period/cohort analysis, orange markets.

INTRODUCTION

Japan is one of the largest foreign markets for U.S. oranges, behind Canada, China (including Hong Kong), and sometimes Korea. The United States is the chief supplier of oranges to the Japanese market, with imports from the United States far exceeding supplies from Japan's own production and imports from other countries. In 2006, the United States shipped almost 100,000 tons of oranges, worth over $70 million, to Japan.

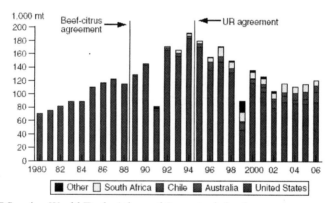

Source: ERS, using World Trade Atlas and Japan trade books.

Figure 1. Japan's imports of oranges

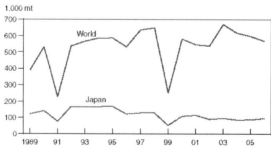

Source: USDA, Foreign Agricultural Service, Foreign Agricultural Trade of the United States database.

Figure 2. U.S. orange export volume

In the late 1980s, Japan was the largest foreign market for U.S. oranges. A key accomplishment of the 1988 Beef-Citrus Agreement between Japan and the United States was to end Japan's quota on orange imports. U.S. orange exports to Japan peaked in 1994-95. However, in recent years, trade volumes have been below the export levels of the late 1980s and early 1990s (figure1), despite lower tariffs negotiated in the Uruguay Round (1995).

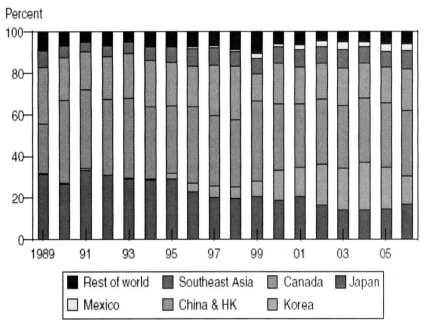

HK = Hong Kong.
Source: USDA, Foreign Agricultural Service, Foreign Agricultural Trade of the United States database.

Figure 3. Share of U.S. orange export volume, by destination

Aggregate U.S. orange exports to all foreign markets have generally been between 500,000 and 700,000 metric tons per year since 1990 (figure 2). Export volume to Japan has decreased somewhat since 1994, so that the Japanese share of U.S. exports has decreased, with Japan falling from the first position in 1989 to third-largest destination in 2006 (and fourth-largest in 2005) (figure 3).

This report investigates Japan's orange market, especially consumption, and factors that affect Japan's imports from the United States.

JAPAN'S CITRUS INDUSTRY

Japan has a long history of citrus production. However, navel orange production is only13,000-18,000 tons annually from about 1,000 hectares (2,500 acres) of orchard. Production of mandarins, called mikan or unshu mandarins in Japan, is much more significant. Japan raises over 1 million tons each year on over 50,000 hectares. Production of other citrus fruits (natsudaidai, hassaku, iyo tangor) is over 200,000 tons each year, from about 13,000 hectares. Aside from the navel oranges, none of these fruits is a conventional orange, and thus less than 20,000 tons of Japanese production competes directly with imported oranges.

Production of most citrus fruits in Japan has been declining. Mikans peaked in 1975 at 3.7 million tons (figure 4), but have since declined to less than one- third of that volume. Production of other citrus has fallen significantly in the last 5 years; navel orange production has declined in each of the last 5 years.

Japanese production has declined in part because of government programs to reduce mikan output after overproduction in the 1970s and in part because of rising farm costs and stagnant sale prices, which have led many farmers to shift land and labor from oranges to other activities. Also, the Beef-Citrus Agreement (implemented in1989-91), ended the orange import quota. The 3-year average mikan production of 1989-9 1 was 1.749 million tons, 20 percent less than the average for 1986-88. This coincided with a rise in orange imports, suggesting that the imported oranges substituted for mikan and other Japanese citrus fruit in that period.

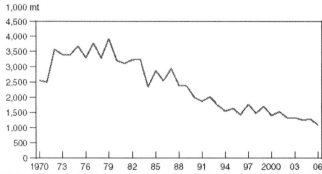

Source: USDA, Foreign Agricultural Service, Production, Supply, and Distribution
    database.

Figure 4. Productions of mikans, Japanese tangerines

Japan's orange imports in recent years have ranged from 100,000 to 120,000 tons. Of this, the United States has supplied about 75 percent. U.S. oranges account for about two-thirds of Japan's market supply, with Japan's own production plus imports from other countries making up the rest.

JAPAN'S IMPORT RULES FOR ORANGES

Before 1989, oranges could be imported into Japan only under an import quota, with a tariff that varied by season. From June 1 through November 30, the tariff was 20 percent of the value of the imported product. From December 1 through May 31, during the peak marketing months for Japan's mikans and oranges, the tariff rose to 40 percent. The Beef-Citrus Agreement raised the quota (above the 126,000-ton level of 1987) according to the following schedule: 148,000 tons in 1988, 170,000 in 1989, and 192,000 tons in 1990. On March 31, 1991—the end of Japan's 1990 fiscal year—the quota was eliminated. Tariffs remained at 40 percent and 20 percent, according to the season, for all countries, including the United States. In the Uruguay Round, Japan agreed to drop the seasonal tariffs to 32 percent (December-May) and 16 percent (June-November) over 1995- 2000, with the final reduction effective March 31, 2001. These tariffs remain in place as of 2008.

The seasonal tariffs provide a strong incentive to import from June to November. Import data show that June imports are usually the highest. April is the second-highest peak (and is within the higher tariff period), but imports always decline in May, presumably because traders delay shipment until the lower tariff applies. After June, Northern Hemisphere oranges are generally out of season. The pattern is the same both for all orange imports (figure 5) and for imports from the United States (figure 6).

For imports from non-U.S. sources, however, the heaviest months are August and September (figure 7). Most non-U.S. imports are from Southern Hemisphere countries (Australia, Chile, and South Africa) which can supply oranges when Japanese and U.S. oranges are out of season. Imports from non-U.S. sources have grown since the mid-1990s (figure 1). In years following poor U.S. harvests, such as 1999 and 2007, imports have also come from Spain and Israel, which have Northern Hemisphere crop calendars, to help offset supply shortages and satisfy consumer demand.

JAPANESE CITRUS CONSUMPTION

Japan's consumption of oranges grew through 1994, offsetting some of the decline in domestic citrus consumption (figure 8). Since 1994, consumption of both oranges and Japanese citrus fruits has declined.

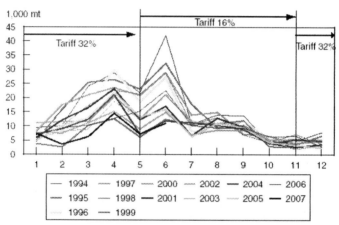

Source: ERS, using World Trade Atlas.

Figure 5. Japan's orange imports peak in April and June

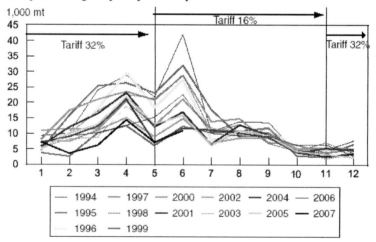

Source: ERS, using World Trade Atlas.

Figure 6. Japan's orange imports from the United States, by month

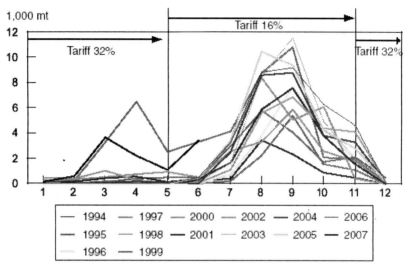

Source: ERS, using World Trade Atlas.

Figure 7. Japan's orange imports from all countries except the United States, by month

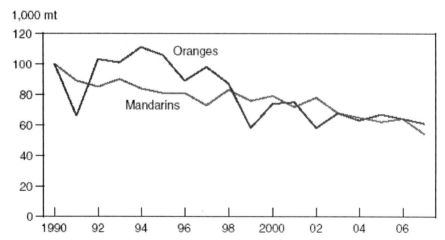

Source: USDA, Foreign Agricultural Service, Production, Supply, and Distribution database.

Figure 8. Japan's consumption of mandarins and oranges; indexed, with 1990 = 100

Japan's Family Income and Expenditure Survey (FIES), a monthly government survey of 8,000 households, records monthly household expenditures on oranges and quantities purchased. At-home consumption accounts for an estimated 70 percent of the total distribution of oranges in Japan (Ito). Orange consumption outside family households is difficult to measure directly. Restaurants, hotels, and other institutional eating places use oranges, and oranges are sometimes given as gifts—it is common in Japan to give large, perfect fruit as gifts. Oranges are also sold at convenience stores. The size and trend of the away-from-home market have not been determined.

Fresh oranges, apart from mandarins and other domestic citrus varieties, were first itemized by FIES in 1987. At-home consumption of oranges increased from 830 grams (g) per person in 1987 to 940 g in 1995 (from 1.8 lbs. to 2.1 lbs.), and then gradually declined to 641 g in 2000 and 533 g in 2005 (1.4 lbs. to 1.2 lbs.). At-home consumption of fresh fruit also declined, from 49.7 kg per person in 1975 (110 lbs.) to 36.4 kg in 1985 (80.2 lbs.), 31.7 kg (69.9 lbs.) in 1995, and 30.5 kg in 2005 (67 lbs.).

FACTORS AFFECTING ORANGE DEMAND IN JAPAN

Economists normally look at price and income effects in assessing factors that shape the demand for specific foods. Over the last 15 years, there has been little change in prices or household incomes in Japan. The general consumer price level, as reflected in the consumer price index (CPI) has been fairly static since 1993. Average household incomes, adjusted for inflation, were about the same in 2006 as in the late 1980s. Incomes rose about 10 percent from 1985 to 1997, then dropped back in the next decade (figure 9).

Throughout 1993-2007, import prices for oranges have been relatively stable, fluctuating in the range of 75-150 yen/kg (29-59 cents/lb.) and only spiking above 150 yen/kg in years when the U.S. orange crop suffered weather-induced losses (1999 and 2007) (figure 10).

Japan's tariff reductions as part of the Uruguay Round Agreement contributed to a slight reduction in the border value of oranges (import unit value plus tariff) after 1995 (figure 11). However, retail prices for fresh oranges, which fell between 1987 and 1993, have shown little tendency to decrease since then (figure 12).[1] Recent research found that orange consumption by Japanese households appears to be responsive to prices (a 1-percent decline in consumer price increased estimated quantity purchased by almost 1.4 percent). But the small change in orange prices (and household income) since 1993 limit any real effect on the purchasing decisions of Japanese households.

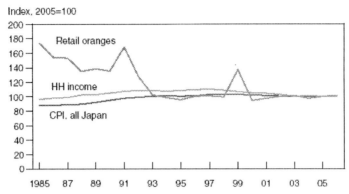

Notes: CPI = Consumer price index. HH = Household.
Source: ERS calculations using data from the Statistics Bureau, Ministry of Internal
Affairs and Communication, Japan.

Figure 9. Japan: prices and incomes, 1985-2006

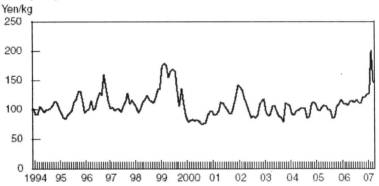

Source: ERS calculations using data from the Statistics Bureau, Ministry of Internal
Affairs and Communication, Japan.

Figure 10. Orange import unit values, CIF, adjusted by CPI; Jan. 1994-Mar. 2007

Another factor that could affect Japan's consumer demand for oranges
would be substitution by a similar fruit. Retail prices for mikan, the closest
substitute product for oranges, have not varied much since 1991 (figure 12),
nor have the relative prices of oranges and mikan. A decline in mikan
consumption appears to coincide with an increase in orange consumption in
1990-94 (figure 8), but orange and mikan consumption have both declined
since then.

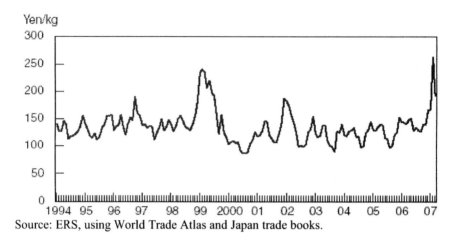

Source: ERS, using World Trade Atlas and Japan trade books.

Figure 11. Import unit values, plus tariff, monthly data, Jan. 1994-March 2007, adjusted by CPIYen/kg.

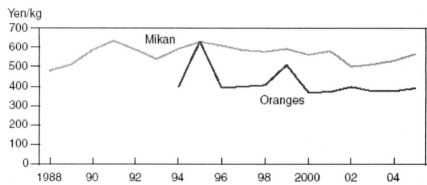

Source: Monthly Statistics of Agriculture, Forestry and Fisheries and Statistical
    Yearbooks of the Ministry of Agriculture, Forestry and Fisheries.

Figure 12. Retail prices of mikan and oranges in Tokyo, deflated by CPI, 1988-2005.

DEMOGRAPHIC EFFECTS ON FOOD CONSUMPTION

Japan has undergone a profound demographic shift in recent decades. Birth rates have fallen, life expectancy has risen, and as a result, Japan's population profile has aged. The birth rate slowed steadily in the 1990s and early 2000s, until the population began to decline in 2005, a phenomenon that is expected to continue.

Japan's 20th century history involved great upheavals and shocks, including urbanization, war, economic depressions, and booms. Generations, or cohorts, of Japanese people born in different decades have had quite different life experiences, and this may affect food consumption patterns.

Studies suggest that fresh fruit consumption rises as individuals age.[2] This means that older people will eat more fresh fruit than younger people. In Japan, the population has aged significantly—while the general population is decreasing, the number of people over 60 is increasing—and this might lead to greater consumption of fresh fruits, like oranges.

Another demographic change is the increase in women's participation in the urban workforce in Japan. This has put pressure on at-home food preparation, which was traditionally done by women. In the case of oranges, this could mean that wives and mothers are less likely to peel oranges (and other fruits) for husbands and children. Women in younger cohorts are more likely to work outside the home than women in older cohorts.

Food consumption in Japan has changed a great deal in the last century. Income and import growth have allowed the Japanese to purchase a wider variety of foods, including some that would otherwise have been unavailable or too expensive in the past. Increased access to imports and greater productivity in the domestic food chain have led to lower prices for some foods. Income and price changes can explain some of the broad shifts in Japanese consumption over the 20th century.

However, the relatively small shifts in income and prices over the last 15 years do not seem highly important for continuing shifts in food consumption in Japan. Demographic effects may explain changes that economic effects do not. Using FIES data, research has assessed changes in Japanese food consumption over time and across a spectrum of age cohorts, finding that fresh fruit consumption has been highest in cohorts born in earlier decades, and lowest in those born most recently. Also, fresh fruit consumption increases with the age of an individual (Mori et al., 2006).

Recent research confirmed the same findings for oranges. As in the case of fresh fruits, the research found that (1) orange consumption is higher, the earlier the person was born (i.e., higher in older cohorts, lower in younger cohorts); and (2) that orange consumption increases as an individual ages, no matter when the person was born, although not at the same rate. In both cases, the effects are progressive and continuous, in general. Each cohort eats fewer oranges than the cohort immediately older than it, and orange consumption increases progressively with the age of an individual.

Older cohorts die out, and are replaced by younger cohorts. Since the older cohorts in Japan (e.g., cohorts born in the 1930s and 1940s) eat more oranges than younger cohorts, as these older cohorts die out, average orange consumption drops. On the other hand, Japan has been rapidly aging, and orange consumption increases with age. The orange consumption of a typical person born in the 1960s, for instance, is higher now than it was 20 years ago. This effect tends to increase average orange consumption.

These two effects—cohort membership and aging—have opposite impacts on orange consumption and tend to offset each other. Thus, the gradual decline in orange consumption to date is not demographically straightforward. Cohort transition (the mortality of cohorts that ate more fruit at any age) in the next decades may have a negative effect on future orange (and fresh fruit) consumption.

OTHER EXPLANATIONS FOR THE SLOW DECLINE OF JAPAN'S ORANGE CONSUMPTION

Demographic research, described above, was able to identify strong cohort and age effects on orange consumption. After these effects were accounted for, the remaining change in orange consumption could be examined for correlation with other factors. The change not explained by the demographic variables showed a downward tendency in the years since 1987 (when the data set began). In other words, orange consumption declined, year to year, in ways not associated with cohort membership or age.

With demographic effects removed, regression techniques tested FIES data to see if household income and consumer prices could explain changes in orange consumption. The tests failed to show significant income effects on orange consumption, (either for the whole period or subperiods within it). Examination of orange purchases by households of varying incomes within single years also found no connection between income level and orange purchases. The price of oranges was, however, a significant variable in the regression. Regressions on the data, without removing the demographic effects, showed roughly similar results, with no significant influence from income changes in recent years.

If demographic changes are important, but with opposite signs that make the net effect neutral, and price and income changes have been small (and, in the case of income, changes do not seem related to orange consumption), what other factors can be responsible for the drop in Japanese orange consumption?

One possibility is a shift from consumption of fresh products toward more convenient processed and packaged products, which are less perishable, and sometimes less expensive per unit (Ito). Regression analysis of orange consumption against expenditures on packaged drinks supports this. Packaged drinks (e.g., bottled green tea) are a significant variable. However, because packaged drink consumption shows a strong positive trend over time, it may just be an indication that some time-related trend (not necessarily packaged drinks themselves) might be causing orange consumption to decline.

However, the consumption of orange juice—a packaged, convenient product widely available in Japan, and a likely substitute for fresh oranges—has not shared in the popularity of some other packaged drink products (see box).

Another possibility is that other fresh fruits are substituting for oranges. Bananas and strawberries are considered easier to consume than oranges, and bananas are also less expensive (Hirata and Ito). In recent years, consumption of these fruits in Japan has not fallen as much as that of oranges and most other fruits. As with processed products, however, research has not established the likelihood of this kind of substitution.

ORANGE JUICE CONSUMPTION IN JAPAN

Orange juice has some of the same taste and nutritional attributes that fresh oranges have, and is very convenient to consume. Orange juice, like oranges, is primarily supplied by imports in Japan.

Orange juice consumption grew rapidly from 1987 to 1994, but has stagnated since. Consumption of competing juices is unlikely to have caused orange juice use to stagnate. Juice from Japanese citrus varieties like mikan is domestically produced. The mikan juice market has declined considerably since the mid- 1980s: consumption in recent years has been under 10,000 metric tons, compared with over 50,000 tons in the mid-1980s. Consumption of grapefruit juice (like orange juice, an import item) grew quickly until 2004 but has slumped since then, reportedly because hurricane damage in exporting areas has reduced supply (Ito, 2004). While grapefruit juice may have substituted for orange juice to some extent, much of its growth may have gone toward a new use: grapefruit juice is frequently mixed with alcohol and sold as a canned or bottled drink (Ito, 2003).

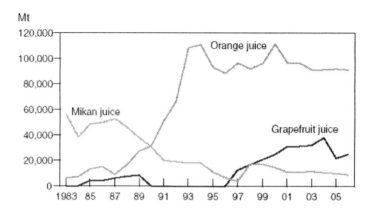

Source: USDA, Foreign Agricultural Service, Production, Supply, and Distribution database

Citrus juice consumption in Japan

The history of orange juice consumption in Japan roughly mirrors that of oranges: growth in the past, followed by stagnation (and some decline), despite Uruguay Round reduction in border barriers. Thus, it is unlikely that orange juice replaced fresh oranges in the Japanese diet.

CONCLUSION

Japan remains an important market for U.S. orange growers, but consumption in Japan has been declining. Income and price changes in Japan have been small in the last decade, and do not appear to have significantly affected orange consumption. Research shows that people born in earlier decades have a stronger preference for oranges and fresh fruits than people born in recent decades. The passage of time thus means that the birth cohorts most likely to eat oranges are dying out. However, individuals eat more oranges as they grow older. Japan's population has shifted to an older age structure, which has helped orange consumption. In the last decade, the two effects have tended to cancel each other out.

Orange consumption has shown a significant tendency to decline each year, for the last decade, after age, cohort, price, and income effects are accounted for. This tendency could continue, although its causes are not well understood. If it does continue, as years pass and the cohort effect becomes stronger (as older cohorts disappear), orange consumption in Japan could suffer steeper drops.

Japan is important to the U.S. orange industry, and any decline in the Japanese market is an unfavorable development. Research shows that Japanese consumption is likely responsive to changes in orange prices. While orange prices in Japan have been fairly steady in recent years, prices might be reduced if Japan lowered its tariffs on orange imports. Another way to reduce prices could be to find ways to reduce the marketing margin that exists between arrival at the port and retail sale. If consumer prices reflected lower tariffs or lower margins, consumption would benefit.

REFERENCES

[1]   Caplan, Lois. (1988). "U.S.-Japan Agricultural Trade Issues," in *Pacific Rim Agriculture and Trade Report*, RS-88-3. United States Department of Agriculture, Economic Research Service. August.

[2]   Coyle, William. (1986). *The 1984 U.S.-Japan Beef and Citrus Understanding: An Evaluation*, FAER 222. United States Department of Agriculture, Economic Research Service. July.

[3]   Ferguson, J. J. (1996). *The Satsuma Tangerine*, Fact Sheet HS-195. Horticultural Sciences Department, Florida Cooperative Extension Service, Institute of Food and Agricultural Sciences, University of Florida. March.

[4]   Government of Japan, Ministry of Internal Affairs and Communication, Statistics Bureau, *Family Income and Expenditure Survey*, various issues, Tokyo.

[5]   Government of Japan, Ministry of Internal Affairs and Communication, Statistics Bureau, Retail Price Survey. *http://www.stat.go.jp/english/data/kouri/index.htm*

[6]   Government of Japan, Ministry of Internal Affairs and Communication, Statistics Bureau, Consumer Price Index. *http://www.stat.go.jp/english/data/cpi/index.htm*

[7]   Government of Japan, *Monthly Statistics of Agriculture, Forestry, and Fisheries*. Various issues.

[8]   Government of Japan. (2005-06). *Statistical Yearbook of the Ministry of Agriculture, Foresty, and Fisheries.*
[9]   Hirata, Jay. (2007). Sunkist Pacific, Ltd. personal communication.
[10]   Ito, Kenzo. (2003). *Japan Citrus Annual Report,* JA3079. United States Department of Agriculture, Foreign Agricultural Service. http://www.fas.usda.gov/gainfiles/200312/146085348.pdf
[11]   Ito, Kenzo. (2004). *Japan Citrus Annual Report,* JA4093. United States Department of Agriculture, Foreign Agricultural Service. http://www.fas.usda.gov/gainfiles/200412/146118376.pdf
[12]   Ito, Kenzo. (2006 and 2007). United States Department of Agriculture, Foreign Agricultural Service. Personal communications.
[13]   Japan Tariff Association, *Japan Exports and Imports, Commodity by Country.* Various issues.
[14]   Mori. (2006). Hiroshi, Kimiko Ishibashi, Dennis Clason, and John Dyck, "Age-Free Income Elasticities of Demand for Foods: New Evidence from Japan," *The Annual Bulletin of Social Science,* Vol. *40,* March, Senshu University, Tokyo, Japan.
[15]   Pollack, Susan L., Biing-Hwan Lin & Jane Allshouse. (2003). *Characteristics of U.S. Orange Consumption,* FTS 305-01. United States Department of Agriculture, Economic Research Service. August. http://www.ers.usda.gov/publications/fts/aug03/fts30501/
[16]   United States Department of Agriculture. (2007). Foreign Agricultural Service, Production, Supply, and Distribution database, accessed Sept.-Dec. http://www.fas.usda.gov/psdonline/
[17]   United States Department of Agriculture. (2007). Foreign Agricultural Service, Foreign Agricultural Trade of the United States (FATUS) database, accessed Sept. *http://www.fas.usda.gov/ ustrade/ USTExFatus. asp?QI=*
[18]   United States Department of Labor, Bureau of Labor Statistics, Consumer Price Index-Average Price Data. http://data.bls.gov/cgi-bin/surveymost?ap
[19]   World Trade Atlas. Official Export and Import Data of Japan. Global Trade Information Service.

End Notes

[1] Tokyo retail orange prices averaged 382 yen/kg in 2003-05, or about $1.56/lb. This contrasts with an average U.S. retail price of $.90/lb. in 2003-2005.
[2] For example, persons over 60 years of age in the United States were found to consume the largest amount of oranges, per person (Pollack et al.).

In: Fruit in Japan: Policies and Issues
Editors: Paul C. Bradley

ISBN: 978-1-61761-115-5
© 2010 Nova Science Publishers, Inc.

Chapter 3

DECLINING ORANGE CONSUMPTION IN JAPAN (GENERATIONAL CHANGES OR SOMETHING ELSE?)

Hiroshi Mori, Dennis Clason, Kimiko Ishibashi, William D. Gorman and John Dyck[*]

ABSTRACT

Japan is a leading market for U.S. oranges. Since 1995, orange consumption in Japan has declined. This report summarizes an analysis of household survey data to assess various factors that may be related to the decline. Consumption of oranges in Japan differs markedly across generations, with younger generations (cohorts) eating fewer oranges than older generations. However, within generations, as individuals in Japan grow older, they eat more oranges. On balance, the effects on consumption associated with aging and birth cohort membership are mostly offsetting. Orange prices affect consumption levels, but household income does not. Even after the analysis accounts for price and demographic variables, a strong downward trend is evident in orange consumption in Japan. Results suggest that orange consumption could decline even more in the future.

[*] Mori is at Senshu University, Japan; Clason and Gorman are at New Mexico State University, Las Cruces; Ishibashi is at the National Center for Agricultural Research, Tsukuba, Japan; and Dyck is at the U.S. Department of Agriculture, Economic Research Service.

Keywords: Japan, oranges, consumption, age/period/cohort analysis

ACKNOWLEDGMENTS

The authors gratefully acknowledge the econometric guidance by Yoshiharu Saegusa of Tokyo Metropolitan University and the comments and suggestions of Bill Coyle, Barry Krissoff, Mary Anne Normile, and Susan Pollack of USDA's Economic Research Service (ERS); Kenzo Ito and Jess Paulson of USDA's Foreign Agricultural Service; Yang Yang of the University of Chicago; Mechel Paggi of Fresno State University; and an anonymous reviewer. Excellent support was provided by the editor, John Weber, and the designer, Wynnice Pointer-Napper, both of USDA, ERS.

SUMMARY

Japan, a leading market for U.S. oranges, has registered declining consumption of oranges, and fresh fruits in general, in recent years. At the same time, Japan's economy has seen little growth and its demographic changes have been profound as its elderly population has increased rapidly as a share of the country's total population. The effects of aging and of generational change on food consumption appear to be major factors affecting orange consumption in Japan.

What Is the Issue?

Since about 1995, orange consumption (in aggregate and per person) has fallen in Japan. One theory attributes that decline to the aging of the population and the fact that younger Japanese eat fewer fresh oranges than older Japanese. Orange prices and income levels are also cited as factors that may be contributing to the dropoff in orange consumption over time. Suppliers to Japan's orange market, largely U.S. growers, may benefit from information on factors triggering the decline as they plan future market strategies in Japan and in such countries as South Korea, which is also characterized by an aging population.

What Did the Study Find?

As individuals in Japan grow older, they eat more oranges; however, older generations of Japanese are being steadily replaced by younger generations who, overall, eat fewer oranges. On balance, the effects on consumption associated with aging and birth cohort membership are mostly offsetting. Prices affect orange consumption in Japan, but household income does not. Even after the analysis accounted for price and demographic variables, a strong downward trend was evident in Japanese orange consumption.

Specific findings include the following:

- Studies show that as Japanese age, they eat more oranges. Thus, today's Japanese youth are likely to increase their orange consumption as they grow older. The aging of Japan's population therefore has a positive effect on orange consumption.
- This analysis estimates, however, that, even in old age, today's younger Japanese will not match the level of orange consumption of today's elderly Japanese. The generational replacement of older birth cohorts by younger birth cohorts therefore has a negative effect on orange consumption in Japan.
- Orange prices in Japan dropped during 1987-95, the first half of the period studied. Orange consumption increased until 1995, perhaps partly in response to the price drops. Price changes since 1995 have been slight. Orange prices have a significant effect on consumption.
- The analysis revealed a strong trend away from orange consumption over time, which was not explained by the effects of demographic variables, prices, or household income.

How Was the Study Conducted?

The study relied on data from Japan's *Family Income and Expenditure Survey*, which collects information on daily expenditures from 9,000 households each month. The survey has gathered information on orange consumption since 1987. The data are reported based on age of the head of the household. Aggregate household orange consumption, rather than consumption by each household member, is reported. The study used detail on the ages of the members of each household to estimate consumption by individual members of different ages. These data were the basis for estimates of age/period/cohort effects. Estimates of consumption per person with the age and cohort (generation) effects netted out were used to investigate "period effects": events, such as price and income changes, that could affect consumption in a given year. These time-series regressions (on own price, income, and a measure of time) determined an estimate of the price elasticity of oranges, as well as a time trend.

Since income elasticity was not significantly different from zero in the time series investigation, various cross-sections of the household data were sorted by income for further study. These cross-sections also failed to show a strong infl uence of income on orange consumption in Japan. Demographic variables were used to project consumption to 2017, to examine the extent to which they could lead to further declines in consumption, in the absence of other changes.

INTRODUCTION

Most fresh oranges (oranges, hereafter) in Japan are imported, and the primary import source is the United States, which accounted for three-quarters of the total in 2004-06. Japan's own citrus production consists principally of a kind of mandarin or tangerine that is not regarded as a close substitute for navel oranges.[1] Japan liberalized its rules for imports of oranges as a result of the 1988 Beef-Citrus agreement with the United States. After a 3-year transition period, Japan replaced existing import quotas with ad valorem tariffs in 1991.[2] The tariffs vary seasonally. Originally set at 20 percent for June through November and 40 percent for December through May, the tariffs were further reduced gradually to 16 percent and 32 percent, respectively, by 2000.

Japan's total imports of oranges, predominantly from the United States, increased steadily from about 111,600 tons in 1985 to 190,400 tons in 1994, the peak year, and then gradually declined to about 136,200 tons in 2000 and 120,900 tons in 2006, respectively (table 1).[3] During this period, Japan fell from the top overseas market for U.S. oranges to the third highest position.

Consumption of oranges in Japan mirrors the product's import history there. The most reliable source of information about orange consumption in Japan is the annual report of the *Family Income and Expenditure Survey* (*FIES*) by Japan's Statistics Bureau (see box, *"Family Income and Expenditure Survey"*). Oranges, apart from mandarins and other domestic citrus varieties, were first itemized in *FIES* in 1987. As measured by *FIES*, per person, at-home consumption of oranges increased from 830 and 737 grams (g) in 1987 and 1988, respectively, to 924-940 g in 1994-96 and then gradually declined to 533-585 g in 2005-06 (table 2). It is estimated that at-home consumption accounts for approximately 70 percent of the total distribution of oranges in Japan.[4]

Table 1. Japan's imports of fresh oranges and country shares

Calendar year	Total	CIF price	From:			
			U.S.	Chile	S. Africa	Australia
	Metric tons	*Yen/kg*	*Metric tons*			
1985	111,635	195.2	110,462	0	0	848
1986	117,300	140.9	115,968	0	0	938
1987	123,425	142.2	122,192	0	0	887
1988	115,347	141.6	114,810	0	0	482
1989	128,372	144.5	125,913	0	0	1,942
1990	145,188	143.7	143,118	0	0	1,833
1991	82,017	220.5	75,161	0	0	3,119
1992	171,701	114.2	166,398	0	1,518	3,366
1993	165,420	104.7	155,728	0	5,151	4,539
1994	190,376	99.7	182,517	0	3,667	3,668
1995	179,960	96.3	169,579	0	4,374	5,866
1996	154,086	111.5	135,683	38	5,905	11,960
1997	171,269	105.3	147,624	87	14,161	8,385
1998	150,470	117.7	131,866	25	9,210	7,357
1999	89,703	152.5	46,204	539	13,846	12,460
2000	136,150	82.3	116,951	1,153	8,547	6,245
2001	126,203	103.7	104,152	3,680	9,337	7,238
2002	103,873	105.1	79,611	4,958	8,028	8,765
2003	117,087	94.9	88,068	6,120	13,276	9,238
2004	112,937	97.2	85,524	10,408	10,216	6,493
2005	115,433	99.6	84,269	11,382	10,960	8,443
2006	120,875	113.0	88,179	9,440	7,714	15,522

Note: CIF means cost, insurance, freight.
Source: USDA, Economic Research Service, using trade data of Japan.

Table 2. Household Purchases of Fresh Oranges in Japan

	Quantity		Real price index[1]
	Per household	Per person	
	Grams		2005= 100
1987	3,046	830	153.33
1988	2,676	737	134.83
1989	2,671	740	138.55
1990	2,882	810	135.28
1991	1,835	514	167.83
1992	2,972	842	128.21
1993	3,114	892	102.30
1994	3,208	924	98.41
1995	3,216	940	95.53
1996	2,575	771	100.60
1997	2,844	851	100.88
1998	2,458	743	99.42
1999	1,257	381	137.18
2000	2,059	622	94.62
2001	1,981	604	97.44
2002	1,733	535	100.00
2003	1,807	561	101.10
2004	1,610	505	97.31
2005	1,691	533	100.00
2006	1,848	585	101.60

[1]Orange Consumer Price Index (CPI) defl ated by CPI for all goods.
Source: USDA, Economic Research Service, using data from *FIES*, various issues.

Like consumption of oranges, consumption of fresh fruit in general has been declining steadily in Japan since the mid-1970s. Per capita at-home consumption of aggregate fresh fruit declined consistently from 49.7 kg in 1975 to 27.8 kg in 2006 (figure 1). Per capita consumption of mandarins declined from 19.97 kg in 1975 to 4.55 kg in 2006.

This report assesses various factors that may be related to the decline in at-home orange consumption in Japan since 1995. It is difficult to attribute the decrease to either an income or a price factor because neither factor has changed much in recent years. Living expenditures per person (a proxy for household income that is reported in *FIES*) in Japan increased slightly from 1987 to 1995 and then remained at about the same level through 2006 (all in constant 2005 yen). The price index for oranges reported in the CPI declined from 153.3 in 1987 to 100.9 in 1996 (defl ated by 2005 aggregate CPI) and remained at the same level since then (figure 2).[5]

The real price index for fresh fruit (defl ated by aggregate CPi) increased slowly from 102.7 in 1975 to 108.1 in 1995 and then slightly decreased to 104.0 in 2006 (2005=100) (figure 3).

FAMILY INCOME AND EXPENDITURE SURVEY

The Family Income and Expenditure Survey, or FIES, is used to depict households' monthly finances and to produce basic statistical data on expenditures of all households by cities, regions, income classes, etc., for planning national economic and social policies. FIES has been conducted since 1946 with ongoing modifications but with time-series consistency maintained as much as possible.

The survey questions approximately 9,000 households, selected by random sampling from all consumer households in all prefectures of Japan, excluding one-person student households. Each household records daily expenditures for 6 months and is then replaced by another household. Each month, one-sixth of the households are replaced.

For many food items, the survey records both expenditure and quantity purchased. In addition, it collects information relating to income and household composition and type. Results are conveyed in monthly and annual reports, published by the Consumer Statistics Division of the Statistics Bureau, Ministry of Internal Affairs and Communication.

On the surface, it appears that at-home consumption of fresh fruit decreased markedly at the same time that income increased substantially (and then remained the same), while fresh fruit consumer prices did not change appreciably over the period. However, a previous study, which analyzed panel data by household types for 96,000 households annually from 1982 to 2001, demonstrated that fresh fruit is an income-positive good (Mori et al., 2006b)—the wealthier the household, the greater the quantity of fresh fruit consumed. The consistent decline in fresh fruit consumption in Japan over the past three decades stems from factors that go beyond household income and price. So, too, does the decrease in orange consumption in the past decade.[6]

Based on recent findings (Mori et al., 2006a; Mori et al., 2006b), this study hypothesizes that the decline in consumption might be at least partially attributed to generational change: more concretely, that today's younger cohorts of Japan's population have moved away from eating fresh fruit, and oranges as well, for unknown reasons (MAFF, 1995).

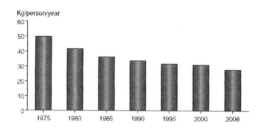

Source: USDA, Economic Research Service, using FIES household survey data.

Figure 1. At-home consumption of fresh fruit in Japan

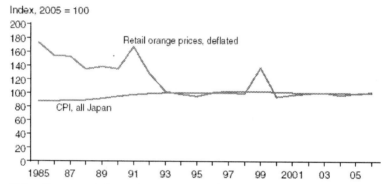

Notes: CPI = Consumer Price Index.
Source: USDA, Economic Research Service, using data from the Statistics Bureau, Ministry of Internal Affairs and Communication, Japan.

Figure 2. Orange prices in Japan

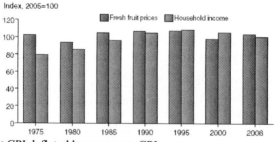

Note: Fresh fruit CPI deflated by aggregate CPI.
Source: USDA, Economic Research Service, using consumer price indexes (CPIs) from Japan's monthly CPI Report.

Figure 3. Real prices of fresh fruit and real household income in Japan

HOUSEHOLD PURCHASES OF ORANGES BY AGE
OF HOUSEHOLD HEAD

Since 1979, *FIES* annual reports have included information on household purchases of various specific goods and services categorized by the age group of the household head (HH). As mentioned earlier, oranges were added to the survey items in 1987.

Table 3. Household purchases of fresh oranges, by age of household head

HH age	1987	1990	1995	2000	HH age	2004	2005	2006
	Grams/year				Grams/year			
~24	1,027	774	627	906				
25-29	1,300	1,136	1,483	880	~29	497	874	445
30-34	2,161	1,789	1,576	879				
35-39	3,163	2,473	2,306	1,504	30-39	765	780	927
40-44	3,299	3,310	2,958	1,962				
45-49	3,427	3,610	4,067	1,933	40-49	1,450	1,310	1,475
50-54	3,553	3,455	3,480	1,938				
55-59	3,046	2,890	3,128	2,663	50-59	1,905	1,879	2,109
60-64	2,880	2,915	3,656	2,297	60-69	1,901	1,957	2,069
65~	3,186	2,694	3,904	2,706	70~	2,312	2,385	2,601
average	3,046	2,882	3,216	2,077	average	1,648	1,691	1,848

Note: HH means household head.

~ means younger than or equal to, before a number, and older than or equal to, after a number.

Source: USDA, Economic Research Service, using data from *FIES*, various issues.

Examination of *FIES* data shows prima facie evidence of two effects on orange consumption (see selected years in table 3): individual aging and cohort effects. During 1987-2006, households with HHs in their forties, fifties, and sixties ate substantially more oranges than those with HHs in their twenties and under age 35. This is a pattern: as households age, they eat more oranges.

Also, data from the 1987 and 1990 surveys show that the households with HHs under age 35 bought fewer oranges than households with older HHs. In 2000-06, the HHs who were under age 35 in 1987 and 1990 were in their forties and their early fifties. They still purchased fewer oranges than house-holds headed by older HHs. This is also a pattern: tracing a cohort diagonally through table 3 reveals that the cohort generally purchases fewer oranges than older cohorts, and more oranges than younger cohorts.

The two patterns pertain to *households* categorized by the age of the HH and may not require further analysis: the *FIES* data give clear indications that cohorts of such households have different purchase levels for oranges, and that each cohort of households increases orange consumption as it ages. However, the household data by HH age group do not necessarily represent the consumption patterns over time by the same cohorts of *individuals*.[7] Individual consumption by age should be separated or derived from household data classified by HH age groups.

DERIVING INDIVIDUAL CONSUMPTION FROM HOUSEHOLD DATA

The *FIES* data provide information on the number of members in the households surveyed and on total household purchases of various foods. The data do not provide information about how much each person in the household consumes. One way to estimate consumption per person would be to divide each household's purchases by the number of people in the household (referred to as "simple division"). Another way would be to use additional information to estimate consumption by individuals of different ages.

To illustrate these two approaches, assume that a three-person household headed by an adult in his/her mid-twenties (age 25) consumed 30 kg of some food, a four-person household headed by a middle-aged adult in his/her late forties (age 47) consumed 60 kg of food, and a three-person household headed by an old adult in his/her mid-sixties (age 65) consumed 80 kg of food.

One could estimate individual consumption by simply dividing household consumption by the number of persons in the household and assigning the result as individual consumption by an individual with the age of the household head. For example, consumption by the young adult age 25 should be $30/3 = 10$ kg; consumption by an adult age 47 should be $60/4 = 15$ kg; and consumption by an older adult age 65 should be $80/3 = 26.7$ kg. However, these results do not take into consideration the age variation among household members.

To show how information about the ages of household members can be used to estimate consumption, consider the households used in the previous example. The first household may comprise two young adults and one infant, the second two adults in their forties and two young adults around age 20, and the third two older adults in their sixties and one adult in his/her thirties (e.g., age 32). Then, the analysis will have a set of equations as follows:

$$2X_{25} + 1 X_0 = 30 \tag{1}$$

$$2X_{47} + 2 X_{20} = 60 \tag{2}$$

$$2X_{65} + 1 X_{32} = 80 \tag{3}$$

where X_i denotes individual consumption by a person i years of age.

The three equations have six unknowns, making it impossible to find a solution. If it can be assumed, however, that infants do not consume this product: $X_0 = 0$; people in their twenties and early thirties eat, on average, about the same amount: $X_{20} = X_{25} = X_{32}$, then one will have the following solutions:

$$2X_{25} = 30 \rightarrow X_{25} = 15 \quad \text{(vs. 10 by simple division)}$$

$$2X_{47} + 2 \times 15 = 60 - X_{47} = (60-30)/2 = 15 \quad \text{(vs. 15 by simple division)}$$

$$2X_{65} + 15 = 80 - X_{65} = (80- 15)/2 = 32.5 \quad \text{(vs. 26.7 by simple division)}$$

The simple division approach implicitly assumes that all members of the household are in the same age group as the HH, or, in an extreme example, that infants eat as much as their parents. The *FIES* panel data of nearly 96,000 households each year provide complete details on the age composition by HH age groups of the households surveyed.[8]

Using simple supporting constraints such as $X_0 = 0$, $X_{20} = X_{25} = X_{32}$, as above, one can obtain more realistic estimates of individual consumption by age from household data than from the simple division approach.

With respect to the supporting constraints, the analysis uses the intuitively natural assumptions of gradual changes between successive age groups (i.e., the difference in consumption between individuals a year apart in age will be approximately zero $(X_i — X_{i+1} \approx 0)$, which cover the entire range of age groups, instead of arbitrary *a priori* assumptions, such as $X_0 \approx 0$, $X_{17} \approx X_{22}$, or $X_7 \approx 0.6 X_{12}$).[9] Individual consumption by age is estimated, minimizing the sum of squared residuals (4) and (5) below.[10]

$$H_j — \sum C_{ij} X_i = E_j \ (i = 1\text{-}16 \ ; j = 1\text{-}10) \tag{4}$$

$$X_k - X_{k+1} = E_k \ (k = 1\text{-}15) \tag{5}$$

where

H_j : consumption by household headed by someone j years of age

C_{ij} : number of individuals of i years of age in household with HH j years of age

X_i : estimated consumption by individuals of i years of age

X_k : estimated consumption by individuals of k years of age

E_j, E_k : residuals

Table 4. Estimates of average individual consumption of fresh oranges in Japan, by age

	Age of consumers (in years)							
	0~4	5~9	10~14	15~19	20~24	25~29	30~34	35~39
	Grams/person/year							
1987	243	372	450	477	472	469	797	1,086
1988	277	390	448	398	381	403	526	1,128
1989	261	342	422	467	502	534	736	776
1990	197	340	486	534	477	439	634	861
1991	121	190	247	255	242	253	383	505
1992	225	361	514	577	594	563	594	813
1993	193	328	486	524	471	471	562	846
1994	104	181	304	414	489	535	597	803
1995	206	301	422	493	510	523	589	774
1996	165	247	337	382	384	392	471	869
1997	136	215	302	338	344	398	542	711
1998	60	112	169	212	265	336	425	778
1999	25	66	105	123	131	155	285	456
2000	139	183	238	278	317	356	410	497
2001	56	108	151	166	170	199	343	493
2002	25	47	87	134	187	243	305	389
2003	108	133	175	217	261	301	316	369
2004	17	53	108	156	192	221	278	375
2005	120	129	157	211	285	344	348	367
	Age of consumers (in years)							
	40~44	45~49	50~54	55~59	60~64	65~69	70~74	75 & older
	Grams/person/year							
1987	1,124	1,210	1,272	1,167	1,163	1,265	1,281	1,207
1988	1,083	988	977	986	1,036	1,056	1,031	936

1989	Age of consumers (in years)							
	40~44	45~49	50~54	55~59	60~64	65~69	70~74	75 & older
1990	1,166	1,268	1,245	1,146	1,202	1,161	1,097	996
1991	623	685	754	765	895	927	915	862
1992	1,133	1,185	1,269	1,157	1,125	1,223	1,238	1,180
1993	1,188	1,281	1,191	1,314	1,390	1,401	1,370	1,281
1994	1,325	1,449	1,516	1,533	1,510	1,581	1,623	1,565
1995	968	1,146	1,217	1,260	1,591	1,716	1,777	1,746
1996	950	1,046	1,028	1,035	1,134	1,354	1,410	1,387
1997	945	1,086	1,147	1,375	1,510	1,601	1,649	1,619
1998	846	931	1,020	1,213	1,332	1,402	1,435	1,406
1999	510	551	558	603	609	617	624	609
2000	609	715	815	910	1,011	1,161	1,325	1,341
2001	627	732	817	910	1,020	1,168	1,318	1,342
2002	496	609	727	849	975	1,090	1,185	1,192
2003	459	553	648	742	847	1,071	1,336	1,392
2004	514	626	724	784	831	929	1,063	1,117
2005	411	505	639	735	821	940	1,082	1,139
2006	552	684	826	880	902	1,004	1,171	1,237

~ means younger than or equal to, before a number, and older than or equal to, after a number.

Source: USDA, Economic Research Service, using Tanaka et al. model with *FIES* household data.

DECOMPOSING INDIVIDUAL CONSUMPTION BY AGE FROM 1987 TO 2006 INTO AGE, COHORT, AND PERIOD EFFECTS

Applying the A/P/C analysis to the estimates of individual consumption by age group in table 4 allows for quantifying age effects for different age groups as such, cohort effects for different birth cohorts as such, and (pure) period effects for different years as such. This analysis uses the Bayesian cohort model first developed by Nakamura (1986) and modified by Clason (Mori, 2001). To overcome the "identification problem" inherent in the linear additive A/P/C model (Mason and Fienberg, 1985), Nakamura introduced *zenshintekihenka* (gradual changes) between successive parameters for the entire range of each of three effects, instead of equality of a few chosen parameters of either age, cohort, or period effects (Rodgers, 1982; Smith, 2004). These identifying constraints of zenshintekihenka are calibrated by hyperparameters ranging from 2^8 to 2^{-8} subject to ABIC (Akaike' s Bayesian

Information Criteria). Mathematically, the Nakamura model can be expressed as follows:

$$X_{it} = B + A_i + PE_t + C_k + E_{it} \tag{6}$$

X_{it} : average consumption by person of i years of age at period t
B: grand mean effect
A_i : age effect to be attributed to age i years old
PE_t : period effect to be attributed to period t
C_k : cohort effect to be attributed to cohort k^{12}
E_{it} : random error

Minimize:

$$\sum [X_{it} - (B + A_i + PE_t + C_k)]^2 \tag{7}$$

Minimize:

$$\frac{1}{\sigma_A^2} \Sigma (A_i - A_{i+1})^2 + \frac{1}{\sigma_P^2} \Sigma (PE_t - PE_{t+1})^2 + \frac{1}{\sigma_C^2} \Sigma (C_k - C_{k+1})^2 \tag{8}$$

$$\Sigma_i A_i = \Sigma_t PE_t = \Sigma_k C_k = 0 \tag{9}$$

In the particular case of oranges, where the differences in consumption per person between the younger and older age groups have widened in recent years (to the order of 1 to 10), the logarithms of X_{it} perform significantly better than the untransformed variables. Table 5 provides estimates of age, period (annual year), and (birth) cohort effects on top of the grand mean effect, all in logs, which explain the changes in individual consumption of oranges by age from 1987 to 2006. For easier visual assessment, estimated cohort parameters in actual numbers are presented in table 6, although the statistical fits are substantially inferior.

The data in table 4 cover all age groups from age 0 to 4 to age 75 and older. Using all the age cells from the youngest to the oldest provides more degrees of freedom in running the least square estimation of equation (7), subject to the identifying constraints of equation (8). However, previous research has shown that estimates of individual consumption by age are less stable for the younger age groups, particularly children under age 15.[13] Including these young age groups could change the size of the period effects and, consequently, other effects in the row. Therefore, the three youngest age groups, 0-4, 5-9, and 10-14, were excluded from this cohort analysis of orange consumption.

Table 5. Changes in individual consumption of fresh oranges, decomposed into age, period, and cohort effects

Age effects: A_i		Period effects: P_t		Cohort effects: C_k	
Age groups (years)	Logarithm	Calendar year	Logarithm	Years born	Logarithm
15-19	-0.1725	1987	0.1123	~ 1912	-0.1453
20-24	-0.2076	1988	0.0378	191 3-17	-0.0783
25-29	-0.2221	1989	0.0693	1918-22	0.0206
30-34	-0.1494	1990	0.0933	1923-27	0.0949
35-39	-0.0534	1991	-0.1232	1928-32	0.1349
40-44	-0.0088	1992	0.1127	1933-37	0.1689
45-49	0.0050	1993	0.1167	1938-42	0.1781
50-54	0.0170	1994	0.1543	1943-47	0.1699
55-59	0.0415	1995	0.1347	1948-52	0.1695
60-64	0.0853	1996	0.0573	1953-57	0.1050
65-69	0.1518	1997	0.0860	1958-62	0.0450
70-74	0.2276	1998	0.0210	1963-67	-0.0065
75 ~	0.2855	1999	-0.2561	1968-72	-0.0289
		2000	-0.0249	1973-77	-0.0614
		2001	-0.0830	1978-82	-0.1606
		2002	-0.1168	1983-87	-0.2599
		2003	-0.0895	1988 ~	-0.3459
		2004	-0.1229		
		2005	-0.0930		
		2006	-0.0862		

Note: Grand mean effects = 0.7912 (original unit: 100 grams).

~ means lower than or equal to, before a number, and older than or equal to, after a number.

Source: Estimates from minimization exercise with original quantity data transformed into logarithms.

DISCUSSION OF AGE, PERIOD, AND COHORT EFFECTS

Results of the A/P/C analysis (tables 5 and 6) indicate that the cohort effects are roughly as important as age effects and that both are substantially more important than "pure" period effects in explaining the changes in individual at-home consumption of oranges during the past decades in Japan. Period effects are the residual after the age and cohort effects are subtracted from the estimates of individual consumption at various ages. Period effects are, thus, not an ordinary time trend but a quantity variable unique to each year with age and cohort effects controlled.

Japanese consumers eat more oranges as they age to the oldest group, 75 and older, whereas those younger than the mid-thirties, in particular, eat substantially fewer oranges than those older than age 60. At the same time, the younger generations born after the mid-1960s are found to consume many fewer oranges than the older generations who were in their late thirties through sixties in the mid-1980s. For easier visual interpretation, the following examples draw on table 6. All consumers can be thought to begin with 782 grams, the grand mean of orange consumption over the whole sample. Membership in the age group 15-19 (column 1, table 6) is estimated to subtract 252 grams (g) from orange consumption, just by virtue of being young. Someone in the group age 75 and older is estimated to add 332 g to consumption. In addition to the other factors, birth cohort membership also changes consumption (column 3, table 6). Membership in the peak orange-eating cohort, born in 1933-37, adds 303g to consumption. Membership in the cohort that eats the least oranges, born in 1978-82, subtracts 233g from consumption. Cohorts born before 1950 tend to eat, on average, 300~500g more oranges than those newer cohorts born after the mid-1970s. Those who will reach their forties in 2017 (born 1968-77) are predicted to eat 400g less oranges than those who were in their forties in the mid-1980s, for example.

The period effects plus the grand mean show annual consumption per person, with age and cohort effects excluded. Comparison of the period effects plus the grand mean with the consumption per person derived by simple division shows that the two results moved in the same directions over time (figure 4). In all years, the period effect plus the grand mean is higher than the result from simple division. The difference is the contribution of the summed age and cohort effects, which must have been negative.[14]

Changes in "pure" period effects derived from the A/P/C analysis seem to be slightly larger in absolute magnitude than those measured in simple consumption per person from the mid-1980s to the mid-1990s on the upward swing, and again somewhat larger in absolute magnitude from the mid-1990s to the mid-2000s on the downward swing. The aging of the population had a positive impact on total consumption, whereas the replacement of the older generations by younger generations had a negative effect (usually with a slightly larger absolute magnitude). On balance, it seems as if the demographic factors—population aging and generational replacement—mostly cancelled each other out in the case of orange consumption in the past two decades. However, will this continue to be the case in the future?

Table 6. Changes in individual consumption of fresh oranges, decomposed into age, period, and cohort effects

Age effects: A_i		Period effects: P_t		Cohort effects: C_k	
Age groups (years)	Grams	Calendar year	Grams	Years born	Grams
15-19	-251.5	1987	146.6	~ 1912	-165.2
20-24	-241.4	1988	7.7	191 3-17	-20.5
25-29	-222.7	1989	41.2	1918-22	186.8
30-34	-143.3	1990	111.5	1923-27	255.0
35-39	-12.7	1991	-222.9	1928-32	301.1
40-44	50.6	1992	141.8	1933-37	302.8
45-49	40.6	1993	183.9	1938-42	256.4
50-54	9.1	1994	306.3	1943-47	181.7
55-59	1.3	1995	242.4	1948-52	133.8
60-64	44.4	1996	75.9	1953-57	-42.9
65-69	138.3	1997	177.8	1958-62	-154.7
70-74	255.4	1998	62.9	1963-67	-209.7
75 ~	331.8	1999	-355.6	1968-72	-189.3
		2000	-63.5	1973-77	-187.3
		2001	-91.7	1978-82	-232.6
		2002	-154.7	1983-87	-184.2
		2003	-138.4	1988 ~	-231.2
		2004	-183.5		
		2005	-175.6		
		2006	-112.2		

Note: Grand mean for the sample is 781.9 grams.

~ means lower than or equal to, before a number, and older than or equal to, after a number.

Source: Estimates based on minimization using original data (not transformed into logarithms).

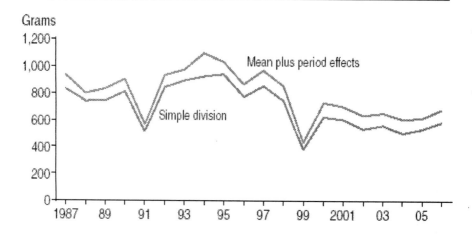

Source: Mean plus period effects from weights reported in table 6 (rather than logarithmic values in table 5); simple division from household observations divided by number of persons in the household.

Figure 4. Orange consumption by individuals in Japan

Cohort effects are quite significant in explaining the changes in orange consumption. Japan's future economy is not easy to predict, but it is quite certain that the older generations born before the mid-20th century—fruit-eating cohorts—will be steadily replaced by newer generations who tend to eat relatively little fresh fruit, for unidentified reasons. To illustrate the implications of cohort changes on orange consumption, the analysis simulates likely individual consumption by age to the year 2017, using the cohort parameters estimated earlier (see table 5 in logs). Table 7 projects individual consumption of oranges by age in 2007 and 2017 (also in 2027, with less confidence), synthesizing estimated cohort parameters: grand mean effect + age effect + period effects + cohort effects (and then transformed into actual numbers in grams). The period effects for the years 2007 and 2017 have not been determined, and it is assumed that they will remain at the 3-year average of 2004, 2005, and 2006. The cohort effects for the "newcomers," who will be ages 15-19 and 20-24 in 2017, have not been estimated, and it is assumed that they will take the same values of the newest two cohorts, who were ages 15-19 and 20-24 in 2006.

Table 7. Individual consumption of fresh oranges by age groups

Age	Actual 1994-96 average	Projected 2007	Projected 2017	Projected 2027
	Grams/person			
15-19	430	164	164	164
20-24	461	167	151	151
25-29	483	203	146	146
30-34	552	302	191	173
35-39	815	406	300	216
40-44	1,081	473	417	263
45-49	1,214	550	464	342
50-54	1,254	649	502	442
55-59	1,276	797	598	504
60-64	1,412	882	760	586
65-69	1,550	1,048	1,028	769
70-74	1,603	1,222	1,225	1,052
75 and up	1,566	1,291	1,426	1,394

Note: Period effects for the future years are assumed constant at the 2004-06 average.
Source: Synthesis of estimated cohort parameters in table 5.

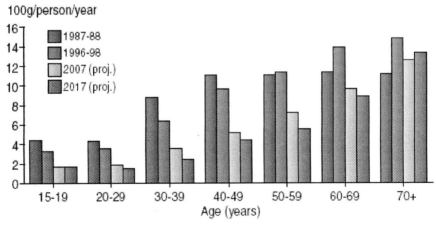

Source: USDA, Economic Research Service.

Figure 5. Individual orange consumption in Japan by age group

In the mid-1980s through the mid-1990s, young Japanese under age 35 consumed on average more than 50 percent fewer oranges than those in their fifties and sixties (figure 5). The disparity between the young and the old in orange consumption has widened since then, with middle-aged adults also moving away from orange consumption. It is predicted that even those in their fifties will eat less than half the oranges than those in their seventies will eat in 2017, if the demographic tendencies observed during the past two decades are assumed to continue. Trends illustrated in figure 5 suggest that the decline in at-home orange consumption since the mid-1990s will accelerate further in the decades to come.

ECONOMIC ANALYSIS OF PERIOD EFFECTS ON ORANGE CONSUMPTION—ARE ORANGES NORMAL GOODS IN JAPAN?

1. Time-series Approach

Japan's orange imports nearly doubled from the mid-1980s to the mid-1990s and then gradually declined to the level of 20 years ago in the mid-2000s (see table 1). Household consumption of oranges as reported in *FIES* followed the same pattern over the period. Did economic variables, such as price and income, infl uence these patterns?[15]

When simple per person consumption of oranges (from *FIES*, using the simple division method) is regressed against real living expenditures per person (as a proxy for income—from *FIES*) and real prices (the price index as reported in CPI surveys), over the years 1987 to 2006, the following estimates are obtained for income and price elasticities:

$$\log (CapQ_t) = 4.71 \ -0.16 \log (CPI\ P_t) \ -0.51 \log (LEX_t) \qquad (10)$$
$$\qquad\qquad (0.58) \quad (-0.41) \qquad\qquad (-0.20) \qquad R^2 = 0.0097$$

where:

$CapQ_t$ = consumption per person in the year t

$CPI\ P_t$ = real price reported by the CPI in the year t (defl ated by aggregate CPI, 2005 = 100)

LEX_t = real living expenditures per person in the year t (defl ated by the aggregate CPI, 2005 = 100)

The numbers in parentheses denote t-values.

The result indicates that the changes in orange consumption per person during 1987-2006 are not explained by the economic factors, own price and household income. This was anticipated, as discussed in an earlier section. Consumption per person fell after the mid-1990s, while both real price and real income remained nearly the same over the corresponding period. When consumption was regressed on real price, and only on the first 10 years, from 1987 to 1996, however, the own price is a significant variable in explaining orange consumption, with the expected negative sign: an own price elasticity around -0.6. The income variable, however, is still not significant when consumption is regressed against it. See the regression equations, (11) and (12).

$$\log (CapQ_t) = 4.20 \quad -0.62 \log (CPI\, P_t)$$
$$(9.57) \quad (-2.97) \qquad\qquad R^2 = 0.5250 \qquad (11)$$

$$\log (CapQ_t) = 1.02 + 0.62 \log (LEX_t)$$
$$(0.21)\ (0.38) \qquad\qquad R^2 = 0.0181 \qquad (12)$$

Data refl ect the 10 years from 1987 to 1996.

It was stated in the previous sections that the changes in orange consumption in Japan for the past two decades could be attributed partially to demographic factors, the aging of the population having a likely positive impact and the replacement of the older cohorts by the new having a negative impact. If the period effects estimated in the cohort analysis (the second columns in tables 5 and 6) represent the net period effects in orange consumption free from the demographic factors, price and income elasticities should be more accurately determined by using the period effects plus the grand mean as a dependent variable in regression analysis like that shown earlier (Mori et al., 2006a). The period effects, unique for each year, should refl ect the infl uence of price and income changes on consumption in that year, as well as of other events or changes.

$$\log (PE_t +GM) = 3.08 \quad -0.08 \log (CPI\, P_t) \quad -0.69 \log (LEX_t) \qquad (13)$$
$$(0.35)\ (-0.20) \qquad\qquad (-0.26) \qquad R^2 = 0.0042$$

where:

PE_t = period effects for the year t, 1987 to 2006
GM = grand mean effect

Results for equation (13) reveal little, other than that the economic variables do not explain changes in orange consumption from the mid-1980s to the mid-2000s, even after accounting for the demographic impacts. When the first 10 years from the mid-1980s to the mid-1990s are examined, the following regression equations, (14) and (15), demonstrate that own price may account for some of the steady increase in orange consumption from 1987 to 1996, at an estimated own price elasticity of around -0.6, whereas income can not be deemed statistically accountable for changes in consumption, at least for the period in question.

$$\log (PE_t + GM) = 2.06 \; -0.57 \log (CPI\ P_t)$$
$$(4.03)\ (-2.34) \qquad\qquad R^2 = 0.4062 \qquad (14)$$

$$\log (PE_t + GM) = 0.21 + 0.22 \log (LEX_t)$$
$$(0.04)\ (0.13) \qquad\qquad R^2 = 0.0020 \qquad (15)$$

where:

PE_t = period effects for the year t, 1987 to 1996
GM = grand mean effect

The same regression efforts show no significant results for the later period of the data, 1997-2006. As mentioned earlier, Japan's economy has been quite stagnant until recently. Household final consumption expenditures changed slightly from 268 trillion yen in Japan fiscal year (JFY) 1995 to 278 trillion yen in JFY2000, and 287 trillion yen in JFY2003 (all in constant 2000 yen). Thus, the steady decline in actual household orange consumption since the mid-1990s and the substantial declines in (pure) period effects from 1994 (second column, tables 5 and 6) are being contrasted to gradual and small shifts in income (recall that the price of oranges remained the same in trend during the past decade since the mid-1990s, figure 2). Factors other than income and/or price effects may have led to the steady reduction in Japan's orange consumption in the past 10 years.

One hypothetical explanation is that the increase in consumption of bottled nonalcoholic drinks replaced the expenditures on fresh fruit. Starting in the mid-1990s, a "PET-bottle culture"[16] took root in Japan, and among young people in particular. Production per capita of PET-bottled or canned tea drinks, mainly Chinese tea and Japanese green tea, soared from under 2 liters in 1985 to 12 liters in 1990, 24 liters in 1995, 35 liters in 2000, and 44 liters in 2005. Over the same period, production (=consumption) of soda drinks and fruit drinks did not change appreciably, whereas that of PET-bottled mineral water followed the same growth pattern as tea drinks (figure 6). The price of a bottle or can of tea drink (350-500 cc) is about the same as the price of one orange, apple, peach, or a large-sized mandarin.

It is difficult to consider PET-bottled soft drinks directly in the category of substitutes for fresh fruit, including oranges. However, it is clear that some forces unfavorable to fresh fruit consumption in the Japanese market have been present during the past decade or so. Adding a simple straight time trend to the regression equations (10) and (13) allows for obtaining the following results of equations, (16) and (17). The results suggest that income elasticities for oranges are not statistically different from zero; that is, oranges are not deemed either an inferior or a normal good, whereas the own-price elasticity is about -1.4, with substantially improved t-values and coefficients of determination.

$$\log{(CapQ_t)} = 8.40 - 1.37 \log{(CPI\,P_t)} + 0.25 \log{(LEX_t)} - 1.42 \log{T}$$
$$(2.47)(-6.57) \qquad\qquad (0.24) \qquad\qquad (-9.16)\ R^2 = 0.8416 \quad (16)$$

$$\log{(PE_t + GM)} = 6.80 - 1.39 \log{(CPI\,P_t)} + 0.21 \log{(LEX_t)} - 1.54 \log{T}$$
$$(1.99)(-6.55) \qquad\qquad (0.20) \qquad\qquad (-9.68)\ R^2 = 0.8547 \quad (17)$$

where:

T = trend dummy starting from 10 at 1987 to increase by 0.5 annually

Data are from 1987 through 2006.

The time trend is quite significant. Its coefficient, -1.5 in equation (17), illustrates the generally declining values of the trend over time. In general, each succeeding year has a smaller period effect or a negative period effect in 1995-2006 (figure 7).

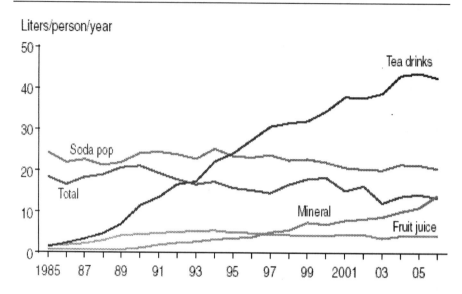

Source: USDA, Economic Research Service, using Japan Soft Drinks Association, Annual Report, various issues.

Figure 6. Bottled beverage production in Japan

2. Cross-sectional Approach

Differences in demand for oranges can also be seen in a cross-section of households at a given time, as well as in averages of households over a peric d of years (as examined earlier). Access to the *FIES* panel data of oranges an d beef classified by household types provides other opportunities to investigate income effects while circumventing the age factors in consumption (Mori et al., 2006b).

This approach uses the data for four major household types: a married couple with HH in the thirties and two children under age 10; a married couple with HH in the forties and two teenagers; a married couple with HH in the fifties and one child in the twenties; and a married couple with HH in the sixties with no dependents. Each household type includes approximately 2-4,000 samples.

Every household reports monthly purchases of various commodities, including oranges, and annual incomes earned during the 12 months prior to the survey month. This analysis uses the 6 months from March through August because the other months are less important for orange consumption in Japan.

Following the lead of Prais and Houthakker,[17] simple double-log regressions of average consumption (monthly purchases) were run against annual incomes by selected income groups, excluding extremely low and high incomes (roughly the bottom and top 5 percent, respectively).

For 1987, oranges are found to be income positive for all household types, with the elasticity ranging from 0.4 to 0.6, significantly different from zero (table 8). In other years, 1999 and 2001, for example, the elasticities vary from zero to greater than 1.0. For 1997, the estimates are found to be insignificant except for the age group of HHs in the sixties. Generally, oranges are estimated as income positive, but statistically the estimates are not conclusive and not consistent over the period 1987-2006.

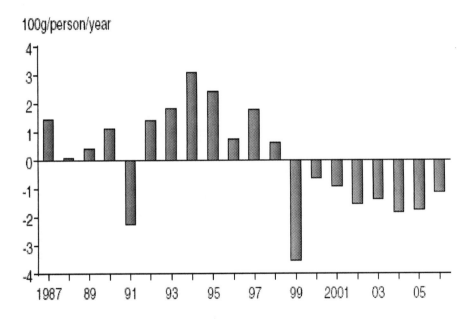

Source: Values are from estimates contained in table 7.

Figure 7. Period effects on orange consumption in Japan

Table 8. Estimates of cross-sectional income elasticities for oranges derived from panel data classified by household types

Ln(Q) = a + b Ln(Y) (1)												
Age of house-hold head	30s			40s			50s			60s		
Age of spouse	30s			40s			50s			60s		
Age of children	Under 10			10-20			20s			0		
Number of children	2			2			1			0		
	Income elasticity	Adjusted R^2	t-value	Income elasticity	Adjusted R^2	t-value	Income elasticity	Adjusted R^2	t-value	Income elasticity	Adjusted R^2	t-value
1987	0.39	0.17	1.84	0.64	0.45	3.55	0.44	0.1	1.68	0.45	0.20	2.02
1989	1.39	0.70	4.47	0.62	0.22	2.11	0.79	0.34	3.23	0.18	0.05	1.32
1991	0.37	0.06	1.40	0.86	0.40	3.02	0.99	0.44	3.11	0.07	-0.06	0.29
1997	0.38	0.02	1.11	0.18	-0.02	0.77	-0.04	-0.05	-0.14	0.65	0.38	3.17
1999	1.25	0.41	3.04	0.06	-0.1	0.08	0.79	-0.04	0.72	0.25	0.07	1.56
2001	1.44	0.61	4.05	1.03	0.24	2.45	-0.04	-0.05	-0.14	0.25	0.03	1.30

Note: Q = monthly household purchase; Y = annual household income; b = income elasticity; t-value is for the parameter b.

Source: USDA, Economic Research Service, using equation (1). Households in each household type are grouped by every 0.5 million yen in annual income.

As an additional approach, all households are classified into income-quintile groups, by four HH types. Within each quintile group, households are arrayed according to the amount of monthly purchases, from zero to 5 kg of oranges in 2001 (households that purchased more than 5 kg of oranges account for less than 0.5 percent of all households in any household type and are deemed "outliers"). In table 9, the share of households reporting zero purchases in any specific month is found in the first row in each household type. The second row provides the average of monthly purchases by those households that reported more than zero consumption.

Table 9. Household monthly fresh orange purchases by income quintile; frequency of zero-purchase households and average amount of monthly purchases by those registering more than zero purchases in each month, March to August, 2001

	Income quintile groups				
	I	II	III	IV	V
	Parents in 30s and two children under 10:				
Zero-purchase households (*percent*)	89.95	90.23	88.69	86.69	85.85
Average amount of purchases by nonzero households (*kg*)	1.023	0.922	1.088	1.113	1.333
	Parents in 40s and two teenagers:				
Zero-purchase households (*percent*)	85.52	80.92	81.63	77.03	84.45
Average amount of purchases by nonzero households (*kg*)	1.064	1.242	1.233	1.191	1.383
	Parents in 50s and one child in 20s:				
Zero-purchase households (percent)	81.13	83.11	81.13	79.8	84.44
Average amount of purchases by nonzero households (*kg*)	1.249	1.169	1.107	1.482	1.106
	Parents in 60s with no dependents:				
Zero-purchase households (*percent*)	86.53	80.53	82.13	81.73	83.2
Average amount of purchases by nonzero households (*kg*)	1.334	1.476	1.434	1.412	1.532

Source: USDA, Economic Research Service, using *FIES* panel data.

Table 10. household monthly beef purchases by income quintile; frequency of zero-purchase households and average amount of monthly purchases by those registering more than zero purchases in each month, 1997

	Income quintile groups				
	I	II	III	IV	V
	Parents in 30s and two children under 10:				
Zero-purchase households (*percent*)	24.3	22.5	18	19.5	15.8
Average amount of purchases by nonzero households (*kg*)	0.887	0.891	0.901	1.021	1.091
	Parents in 40s and two teenagers:				
Zero-purchase households (*percent*)	11.3	7.2	9.5	9.5	9.5
Average amount of purchases by nonzero households (*kg*)	1.633	1.493	1.599	1.674	1.787
	Parents in 50s and one child in 20s:				
Zero-purchase households (*percent*)	14.5	15.2	14.6	14.6	15.4
Average amount of purchases by nonzero households (*kg*)	1.215	1.148	1.147	1.134	1.175
	Parents in 60s with no dependents:				
Zero-purchase households (*percent*)	38.9	34	32.6	30.8	26.5
Average amount of purchases by nonzero households (*kg*)	0.792	0.76	0.786	0.822	0.937

Source: USDA, Economic Research Service, using *FIES* panel data.

Table 10 provides the cross-sectional findings enumerated in the same manner for beef in 1997.[18] The percentages of zero (monthly) purchases are 10 to 30 percent, substantially smaller than the case of oranges, which average slightly over 80 percent. The differences between the two cases are striking: first, the percentage of zero purchases tends to decline as the group income increases for beef, whereas the zero percentage does not vary by income group for oranges; second, the average size of monthly purchases by those households which recorded purchases greater than zero tends to increase as the group income increases for beef, whereas that for oranges does not vary by income group.

It may be safe to conclude that beef should be truly a "normal" good in two senses: as income increases, more households tend to buy beef and in greater amount on average. In contrast, oranges are not income-related in any sense: the share of households that purchases oranges may not respond positively to the increase in average income of the group, and the mean of household purchases may not increase as income increases. Cross- sectionally, oranges are deemed to be neither a "normal" nor an "inferior" good in terms of economics.

CONCLUSIONS

The orange market in Japan, largely supplied by U.S. growers, has declined since the mid-1990s. Declining consumption per person is difficult to explain using the effects of income and price changes. Consumption per person, defined as simple division of household consumption of oranges by all household members, ignores differences in age, which may affect consumption. In fact, it is readily apparent that both age and cohort membership affect household orange consumption in Japan.

Both cohort and age effects are found to be strong. As individuals age, they generally eat more oranges per year, according to this analysis. Membership in a decadal birth cohort that was born in the first half of the 20th century is associated with relatively high levels of orange consumption; decadal birth cohorts since the mid-20th century have consumed progressively fewer oranges. These two demographic effects have tended to cancel each other out.

The Japanese market is quite important to U.S. producers. This investigation indicates that consumption of oranges may decline further, both as a result of an unexplained, but strong, negative time trend and as a result of generational changes: as today's older cohorts die off, U.S. oranges are losing their best customers.

It appears that the price of oranges does matter to consumers in Japan. Reducing or eliminating tariffs could lead to lower orange prices in Japan. Also, reductions in the margin between import and retail prices would lead to lower retail prices. Substantially reduced retail prices of oranges might appeal particularly to young households, which typically have lower incomes among all households in the Japanese labor market.

Japan's household consumption data provide an excellent opportunity to study consumer behavior. In the case of consumption of fresh fruits, including oranges, it appears that systematic, age-related changes are underway that lead to lower consumption of foods that are generally regarded as good for health.

Further studies of consumption of fresh fruits and other foods in other countries may also show strong effects of age and cohort membership. Studies establishing the presence and extent of such effects can provide the basis for consumer surveys that examine why these effects occur and what marketing steps might be effective in addressing them.

REFERENCES

[1]   Deaton, A. & Paxson, C. (2000). "Growth and Saving Among Individuals and Households," *Review of Economics and Statistics*, *82*(2), 212-25.

[2]   Deaton, A. & Paxson, C. (1994). "Saving, Growth, and Aging in Taiwan," in *Studies in the Economics of Aging*, D.A. Wise (ed.), Chicago University Press, 331-57.

[3]   Government of Japan, Bureau of Statistics. *Family Income and Expenditure Survey*, various issues, Tokyo.

[4]   Government of Japan. (2006). Ministry of Agriculture, Forestry, and Fisheries (MAFF). Fruit and Flowers Division, personal communication.

[5]   Government of Japan. (1995). Ministry of Agriculture, Forestry, and Fisheries. *White Paper on Agriculture for 1994*, Tokyo.

[6]   Hendrickson, M. Lewis, H. Mori, & Wm. D. Gorman (2001). "Estimating Japanese At-Home Food Consumption by Age Groups While Controlling for Income Effects," H. Mori (ed.), *Cohort Analysis of Japanese Food Consumption*, Tokyo, Senshu University Press.

[7]   Ishibashi, Kimiko. (2007a). "Changes in Food Consumption Structures and Projections of Future Food Demand (shokuryo shouhikouzo no henka karamita shokuryo jyuyodoukou to jyuyo yosoku)," *Chouki Kinyuu*, No. 99, November, Agriculture, Forestry and Fisheries Finance Corporation, p. 61, in Japanese.

[8]   Ishibashi, Kimiko. (2007b). "Household Food Consumption by Age, Sex and Household Type (nenrei/seibetsu/setairuikeide mita kateideno shokuryou shouhi jittai)," *Report on Agriculture, Forestry, Fisheries, Food and Consumer, 2007-10,* Agriculture, Forestry and Fisheries Finance Corporation, p. 33, in Japanese.

[9]   Ito, Kenzo. (2006). Specialist, American Embassy, Tokyo, personal communication.

[10]   Mason, W. M. & Fienberg, S. E. (eds.). (1985). *Cohort Analysis in Social Research: Beyond the Identification Problem*, New York, SpringerVerlag.

[11] Mori, H. & Inaba, T. (1997). "Estimating Individual Fresh Fruit Consumption by Age from Household Data, 1979 to 1994," *Journal of Rural Economics*, *69*(3), 175-85.

[12] Mori, H., Clason, D. L. & Lillywhite, J. (2006a). "Estimating Price and Income Elasticities for Foods in the Presence of Age-Cohort Effects," *Agribusiness: an International Journal*, *22*(2), 201-217.

[13] Mori, Hiroshi (ed.). (2001). *Cohort Analysis of Japanese Food Consumption—New and Old Generations*, Tokyo, Senshu University Press.

[14] Mori, Hiroshi, John Dyck, Susan Pollack & Kimiko Ishibashi. (2008). *The Japanese Market for Oranges,* U.S. Department of Agriculture, Economic Research Service, Outlook Report No. FTS-33001, March.

[15] Mori, H., Ishibashi, K., Clason, D. L. & Dyck, J. (2006b). "Age-Free Income Elasticities of Demand for Foods: New Evidence From Japan," *Annual Bulletin of Social Science*, No. 40, Senshu University, 17-47.

[16] Nakamura, Takashi. (1986). "Bayesian Cohort Models for General Cohort Tables," *Annals of the Institute of Statistical Mathematics*, 38, 353-370.

[17] Prais, S. J. & Houthakker, H. S. (1955). *The Analysis of Family Budgets*, University Press, Cambridge, England.

[18] Rodgers, W. L. (1982). "Estimable Functions of Age, Period, and Cohort Effects," *American Sociological Review*, *47*(6), 774-787.

[19] Smith, L. Herbert. (2004). "Response: Cohort Analysis Redux," *Sociological Methodology*, Vol. *34*, American Sociological Association, 111-119.

[20] Tanaka, M., Mori, H. & Inaba, T. (2004). "Re-estimating per Capita Individual Consumption by Age from Household Data," *Japanese Journal of Rural Economics*, Vol. *6*, 20-30.

[21] Yang, Y., Fu, W. J. & Land, K. C. (2004). "A Methodological Comparison of Age-Period-Cohort Models: The Intrinsic Estimator and Conventional Generalized Linear Models," *Sociological Methodology*, Vol. *34*, American Sociological Association, 75-110.

End Notes

[1] Partly because of seasonal import tariffs, which are higher in December- May, there are strong seasonal differences in citrus consumption in Japan, with most mandarins consumed in October-February, and most navel oranges consumed in March-September. For more information, see Mori et al., 2008.

[2] See Mori et al., 2008.

[3] Declines in imports in 1991 and 1999 refl ected short supplies caused by harvest failures in California.

[4] Ito, 2006: at-home consumption (*FIES* per person consumption times total population) is estimated at 60-65 percent of imports. Ito surmises that 10-15 percent of total imports may not be suitable for normal fresh marketing due to spoilage, and the like. At-home consumption of the marketable share would thus be about 70 percent.

[5] Price spikes in 1991 and 1999 reflected short supplies caused by harvest failures in California.

[6] See "Economic Analysis of Period Effects on Orange Consumption—Are Oranges Normal Goods in Japan?", on page 14, for an economic analysis of orange consumption.

[7] Deaton and Paxson, 1994; Deaton and Paxson, 2000.

[8] These data are not usually available to the public but were made available for this study. The actual family age compositions by HH age groups are made public only partially in *FIES* annual reports, and, if then, on a sporadic basis. The data are much more complex than that illustrated in the example, and thus, may require difficult supporting constraints.

[9] Hendrickson et al., 2001, pp. 107-08.

[10] Mori and Inaba, 1997; Tanaka et al., 2004.

[11] Estimates for younger age groups, the early twenties and the late twenties in particular, are less stable or less dependable than those for older age groups above the thirties because the HH age groups under age 25 and age 25-29 (in recent years) are small in sample size. The estimates of nonadults under age 20 are also not dependable because, unlike a married couple of two adults in the same age brackets, these individuals do not represent the principal components of age matrices of family structure by HH age groups, C_{ij}, in equation (4). Also, they are more prone to be subject to the supporting constraints of gradual changes between successive age groups (i.e., $X_{17} - X_{22} \approx 0$, $X_{12} - X_{17} \approx 0$, etc.) in deriving individual consumption from the household data organized by HH age groups.

[12] In the case of a standard cohort table, in which the survey period matches the age classification, a cohort in a particular age cell moves down to the next age cell at the subsequent survey period—that is, every cohort follows a diagonal line in the table. In the data used by this study, age is classified by 5-year intervals, and data are available for each year (period) from 1987 to 2006. A moving average operator in the design matrix apportions the cohorts into annual age cells. Consider cohort k in the ith age cell in 1987, for example. It is assumed that 20 percent of cohort k has moved to the next age cell ($i + 1$) in 1988 and that the ith age cell in 1988 comprises 20 percent of the next younger cohort ($k + 1$) and 80 percent of the remaining cohort k. Nakamura (1986) pioneered this general cohort analysis, and further details on the methods used in the current study are given in chapter 10, "Age in Food Demand Analysis" (pp. 323-34 in particular) in Mori (ed.), *Cohort Analysis of Japanese Food Consumption* (2001).

[13] For example, Ishibashi, in two publications from 2007, found several cases of negative consumption estimates for the younger age groups, using methods and data similar to those used in this study. Also, for the case of ages 0-9, in particular, see Mori, Hiroshi, and William D. Gorman, "A Cohort Analysis of Japanese Food Consumption—Old and New Generations," chapter 8 in Mori (ed.), 2001, pp. 265-6.

[14] The comparison is made with the estimates using actual weights reported in table 6, rather than results from estimation using logarithms in table 5.

[15] Prices of possible substitutes were not included because most fresh fruits, including the domestically produced mandarin oranges, showed declines in consumption similar to or greater than those of oranges over this period, and because the annual series of observations is relatively short, making estimation with a larger number of variables difficult. See Mori et al., 2008, for further discussion of possible substitutes for oranges.

[16] PET is an acronym for polyethylene terephthalate. PET bottles are commonly referred to as plastic bottles.

[17] See pp. 79-108.

[18] The year 2001 was not selected for beef because of outbreaks of BSE, or bovine spongiform encephalopathy, that year.

CHAPTER SOURCES

The following chapters have been previously published:

Chapter 1 is an edited, excerpted and augmented edition of an United States Department of agriculture publication, a report from the Economic Research Service FTS-341-01 dated April 2010.

Chapter 2 is an edited, excerpted and augmented edition of an United States Department of agriculture publication, a report from the Economic Research Service FTS-330-01 dated March 2008.

Chapter 3 is an edited, excerpted and augmented edition of an United States Department of agriculture publication, a report from the Economic Research Service dated February 2009.

INDEX

A

accounting, 68
adjustment, 7, 11
Afghanistan, 29
Africa, 29, 51
aging population, 8, 48
agricultural market, 2
agriculture, 4, 8, 9, 29
apples, 2, 10, 11, 17, 19, 21, 23, 26, 30
Asia, 29
assessment, 61
authors, 1, 31, 48

B

Bahrain, 29
Bangladesh, 29
barriers, 1, 14, 21, 24, 44
beef, 70, 76, 80
Bhutan, 29
birth rate, 40
Burma, 29

C

Cambodia, 29
category a, 16
Census, 7
challenges, 9
Chile, 17, 35, 51
China, 23, 29, 32
chlorine, 19
City, 30
classification, 80
composition, 57
conference, 25
consolidation, 24
consumer demand, 35, 39
consumer price index, 38, 54
consumption patterns, 41, 56
correlation, 42
cost, 10, 11, 14, 19, 21, 51
country of origin, 5
covering, 12
crops, 2, 7, 10, 11, 19, 24, 29
culture, 69

D

data set, 42
database, 3, 6, 32, 33, 34, 37, 44, 46
demographic change, 41, 42, 48
demographic factors, 63, 67
Department of Agriculture, 24, 25, 26, 45, 46, 47, 79
dependent variable, 68
destination, 33
developed countries, 2, 17, 29
developing countries, 16, 17
diet, 44
domestic demand, 7
drought, 13

E

East Timor, 29
economy, 48, 63, 69
Education, 13
elderly population, 48
encephalopathy, 80
encouragement, 14
England, 79
equality, 60
exchange rate, 10, 27, 28
exercise, 61
expenditures, 4, 37, 43, 49, 52, 53, 67, 69
exports, 2, 3, 8, 19, 23, 28, 31, 33

F

farm income, vii, 1, 9, 26
farm size, 7
farmers, 4, 7, 8, 9, 10, 11, 12, 13, 14, 21, 23,
    24, 27, 34
farmland, 7, 9
farms, 4, 7, 8, 12
FAS, 20, 29
financial support, 24
freedom, 62
frost, 12
fruits, vii, 1, 2, 4, 5, 9, 10, 12, 14, 17, 21,
    23, 24, 25, 28, 29, 34, 36, 41, 43, 44, 48,
    77, 80
funding, 9

G

global trade, vii, 2
goods and services, 55
guidance, 48

H

Haiti, 29
highways, 14
historical reason, 4

Hong Kong, 29, 32, 33
hotels, 38
household composition, 53
household income, 38, 42, 47, 49, 52, 53,
    54, 67, 73

I

identification problem, 60
impacts, 30, 42, 68
import prices, 38
import tariffs, 79
imports, 1, 4, 5, 14, 17, 19, 20, 21, 22, 23,
    24, 29, 30, 31, 32, 33, 34, 35, 36, 37, 41,
    43, 45, 50, 51, 66, 79
inclusion, 29
income effects, 38, 42, 44, 70
infants, 57
inflation, 3, 38
insects, 12
inspections, 19
Israel, 29, 35
issues, 7, 9, 17, 23, 25, 26, 27, 45, 46, 52,
    55, 70, 78

K

Korea, 17, 29, 32
Kuwait, 29

L

Laos, 29
leadership, 9
life expectancy, 40
life experiences, 41
local government, 11, 14, 26
lower prices, 23, 24, 41

M

management, 1, 8, 9, 24, 26, 28
Mandarin, 6

marketing, 9, 11, 22, 24, 35, 45, 78, 80
matrix, 80
Mediterranean, 18
melon, 18
membership, 42, 47, 49, 62, 77, 78
meter, 19
Mexico, 2, 47
mineral water, 69

N

natural hazards, 23
Nepal, 29
New York, v
New Zealand, 17
North America, 28
North Korea, 29

O

obstacles, 14
Oceania, 29
old age, 49
opportunities, 70
overproduction, 34
ownership, 7
ownership structure, 7

P

Pacific, 45
parameter, 73
permission, v
personal communication, 45, 78
pests, 12, 17
Philippines, 4, 30
plants, 29
port of entry, 19, 20
ports, 17
price changes, viii, 31, 41, 44, 77
price effect, 69
price elasticity, 30, 50, 67, 68, 69
price index, 2, 5, 39, 52, 53, 67
prima facie, 55

producers, 4, 7, 11, 12, 24, 77
production targets, 11
project, 11, 26, 27, 50
protection systems, 17
public interest, 13

Q

Qatar, 29
quotas, 50

R

rainfall, 13
real income, 67
recall, 69
recommendations, v
regression, 42, 67, 68, 69
regression analysis, 68
regression equation, 67, 68, 69
relative prices, 39
replacement, 49, 63, 68
residuals, 57, 58
respect, 57
restaurants, 2
restructuring, 11
retail, 21, 22, 23, 30, 38, 45, 46, 77
revenue, 13
rights, v

S

sea level, 2
senses, 76
shape, 38
shortage, 4
signs, 42
Singapore, 29
South Africa, 35
South Korea, 48
Spain, 35
Spring, 18
stabilization, 9, 28
statistics, 5, 22

subsidy, 9, 11, 12, 26, 28
substitutes, 69, 80
substitution, 39, 43
survey, 13, 30, 37, 47, 49, 53, 54, 55, 59,
　　71, 80

T

Taiwan, 29, 78
tariff, 3, 6, 16, 17, 21, 29, 30, 35, 38, 40
time series, 50
total product, 12
trading partner, 19
transition period, 50
transport, 22, 23
transportation, 29

U

United Arab Emirates, 29
United Nations, 6
urban areas, 22

urbanization, 41
Uruguay, 33, 35, 38, 44

V

vegetables, 14
volatility, 7

W

waterways, 10
wholesale, 2
World Trade Organization, vii, 2
World War I, 7

Y

Yemen, 29
young adults, 56, 59